Diary of a
Confederate Soldier

DIARY OF A CONFEDERATE SOLDIER:

John S. Jackman of the Orphan Brigade

Edited by William C. Davis

University of South Carolina Press

Copyright © University of South Carolina 1990

Published in Columbia, South Carolina, by the
University of South Carolina Press

Manufactured in the United States of America

Library of Congress Cataloging-in-Publication Data

Jackman, John S., 1841–1912.
   Diary of a Confederate soldier: John S. Jackman of the Orphan
Brigade / by John S. Jackman : edited by William C. Davis.
      p.   cm.—(American military history)
   Includes bibliographical references and index.
   ISBN 0–87249–695–3
   1. Jackman, John S., 1841–1912—Diaries. 2. United States—
History—Civil War, 1861–1865—Personal narratives, Confederate.
3. Confederate States of America. Army. Kentucky Brigade, First—
Biography. 4. Kentucky—History—Civil War, 1861–1865—Personal
narratives. 5. Soldiers—Kentucky—Diaries.   I. Davis, William C.,
1946– . II. Title. III. Series: American military history
(Columbia, S.C.)
E564.5 1st.J33 1990
973.7′469—dc20   90–12431
                                                  CIP

Contents

Diary of a
Confederate Soldier

Introduction

"Nearly four years have passed," John Jackman wrote in the spring
of 1865 as he looked back upon his service for the Confederacy. What
years they had been, especially for a young man who left home for
adventure, and wound up taking part in the greatest experience of
his generation. For those young men who went to war in 1861 and
the years following, the sights and sounds and the hardships and
perils of America's bloodiest war became ever after a part of their
lives.

Then and thereafter, most of the interest and attention was fo-
cused upon the armies and events in Virginia, on the one hundred-
mile stretch of territory that separated the capitals of Union and
Confederacy. But there was another war, spread over hundreds of
thousands of square miles between the Mississippi River and the Ap-
palachians. There, in what was then called the West, great armies
vied for whole states, and there, historians will argue, the war was
won and lost.

The units composing those western armies are, like their battles
and campaigns, less remembered than their Virginia counterparts.
Yet even before the conflict was ended, one Rebel command stood
apart and has remained, for more than a century since, perhaps the
most storied group of men of all those that formed the great Army of
Tennessee. During the war they were known to themselves and their
comrades as the First Kentucky Brigade. But even before the war's

end they acquired another name, one their first historian likened to "a kind of title of nobility": the Orphan Brigade.[1]

Theirs was a story that few could match and none surpass. While their organization varied in the early years, for most of the war the brigade consisted of the 2d, 4th, 5th, 6th, and 9th Kentucky Infantry and a battery of artillery. Raised out of Kentucky, which never seceded, the brigade had to form its regiments in Tennessee in the fall of 1861, then march back into Kentucky when that state abandoned neutrality, to continue recruiting and complete its organization. Here John Jackman joined what was to become the 9th Kentucky, and he was with the brigade when the Confederates abandoned Bowling Green in February 1862. Of more than four thousand who marched out of Kentucky that February, barely six hundred were left at the end of the war.[2]

The balance were buried all across the South. From their first battle at Shiloh, they marched on through the summer fighting at Vicksburg, then to Baton Rouge, then back up through Tennessee to Murfreesboro, where some say they first received the sobriquet "orphans" in battle. They were off again to Vicksburg in the summer of 1863, back to Georgia for the Battle of Chickamauga, into Tennessee for the disaster at Missionary Ridge, clear across Georgia in every fight of the Atlanta campaign, and then resisting Sherman's march to the sea. When finally there were too few of them left for an infantry brigade, they were given horses and made into mounted infantry as they continued to resist Sherman right up to the last days of the war. As coincidence would have it, they finally took their parole in Washington, Georgia, just as President Jefferson Davis and his cabinet passed through on their desperate attempt to escape the crumbling Confederacy. There was very little these Kentuckians missed.

Where battle was thickest, there they were to be found. When a retreat needed to be covered, that was their post. Whether in a hopeless, desperate charge at Stones River or in a relentlessly victorious assault at Chickamauga, they always stood out. Army commanders pronounced them the finest in the service. Their foes even paid tribute to their valor. And the citizens of the Confederacy looked

---

1. Ed Porter Thompson, *History of the Orphan Brigade* (Louisville, Ky.: L. N. Thompson, 1898). p. 21 (cited hereinafter as Thompson).
2. William C. Davis, *The Orphan Brigade* (New York: Doubleday, 1980), p. 270 (cited hereinafter as Davis).

upon them with a loving admiration mixed with a bit of terror of the "wild Kentuckians." Not a little self-important, they had no doubt their historian was right in that business about titles of nobility.

Off the battlefield, they stood out as well. They formed their own debating society, started a glee club to serenade the camps, put on amateur theatricals, built a brigade library, and even elected their own representatives to the Confederate Congress. It is hardly a surprise that Ed Porter Thompson, a captain in Company E, 6th Kentucky, believed his unit sufficiently important to posterity that he began work on his brigade history several months before the war was over.[3]

Indeed, it is not at all improbable that the Kentucky Brigade may have been the most literate and educated in the Army of Tennessee. If so, then it is all the more ironic that so little has survived from the pens of the soldiers themselves. Of letters written by the Kentuckians, no more than a small handful is known to exist, due in great measure to the fact that for all but a few months of the war they were entirely cut off from home and kindred, Kentucky being behind enemy lines. Two officers, Thompson and George B. Hodge, published histories of the brigade shortly after the war, and two enlisted men published much later brief memoirs of their service. Only one completely contemporaneous enlisted man's diary, the year-long journal of Squire Helm Bush of the 6th Kentucky, is known. Indeed, until now the fullest and most complete portrait of the private soldier's war to come from the brigade was not a diary at all, nor even strictly a memoir. John W. Green's recollections of service in Company B, 9th Kentucky, are, rather, a kind of pastiche based on wartime notes, the reminiscences of others, and stories he read in the postwar press and worked into his own narrative, with himself the protagonist. As edited by the late Albert Kirwan, *Johnny Green of the Orphan Brigade* does provide an excellent portrait of the life and spirit of the Orphans, but it is about as far removed from being a contemporaneous source as possible.

All of which makes it the more fortunate that there was another boy of Company B, 9th Kentucky, who did keep a genuine diary. Indeed, he was a friend of John Green's and the two spent one winter together sharing the same hut and making notes about each other. As a result, the journal of John Jackman is the longest, most informa-

_____
3. Thompson, p. 21.

tive, and most unvarnished account that we have to show us what service with the Orphan Brigade was really like.

John S. Jackman was decidedly out of the ordinary for a Confederate enlisted man, though not unusual among his fellow Kentuckians. Born in December 1841 in Carroll County, Kentucky, to an educated family, he attended public schools and, according to his mess mate Green, was a carpenter before turning to school teaching.[4] Certain it is by the evidence of his journal that young Jackman knew literature, both modern and the classics, had at least some familiarity with Latin, was no stranger to mathematics and music, and possessed a better command of spelling and grammar than most of either the twentieth century or his own era.[5]

By the time war came, Jackman and his family had moved to the vicinity of Bardstown, Kentucky, and it was from their home on September 26, 1861, that he walked out one day, "to get the daily papers," and wound up going off to war for three and one-half years.

The young man who said good-bye to his parents that day was blue-eyed and fair complected, with thin, dark hair atop his five-foot eight-inch frame.[6] No wartime photograph of him has been found, but judging from a portrait made thirty or more years later, his was a pleasant, smiling visage despite his often sickly nature. Indeed, posterity can be thankful that Jackman's health was frail, for just as his educational attainments frequently resulted in his being detailed to headquarters as adjutant's clerk, so did his poor health often keep him off the battlefield and out of harm's path. As a result, Jackman was in a position to observe much and to live to record it in his journal.

Young Jackman's first battle was Shiloh in April 1862, and thereafter he was never away from the brigade except when ill. He marched with the Orphans to Vicksburg that summer, but was too ill to go with them to Baton Rouge in August. Soon afterward, however, he accompanied the command northward to Knoxville and Murfreesboro, saw the carnage of Stones River, then came back to Mississippi in the summer of 1863 before turning right around and going back

---

4. Albert D. Kirwan, ed., *Johnny Green of the Orphan Brigade* (Lexington, Ky.: University Press of Kentucky, 1956), p. 118 (cited hereinafter as Kirwan).

5. J. Stoddard Johnston, *Kentucky*, volume XI of *Confederate Military History*, ed. Clement A. Evans (Atlanta: Confederate Publishing Co., 1899), p. 405; H. Levin, ed., *The Lawyers and Lawmakers of Kentucky* (Chicago: N.p., 1897), p. 302.

6. John S. Jackman, Oath of Allegiance, May 6, 1865, in John S. Jackman Compiled Service Record, Record Group 109, National Archives, Washington, D.C.

northeast to Chickamauga and Chattanooga. There, like so many of his brethren, he took part in the religious revival that swept the Army of Tennessee in the winter of 1863–1864. Then he marched off again on the road to Atlanta. He did not make it all the way, however, for on June 14, 1864, at Pine Mountain, a shell fragment struck him on the head, inflicting what his later symptoms would reveal as a severe concussion. For the next several months Jackman convalesced in central Georgia before rejoining the remnant of the brigade, now partly mounted. Still frail—indeed, he would suffer some complications from the injury for the rest of his life, as it left his skull slightly depressed—he was detailed to take the brigade archives to safety at Washington, Georgia, and there he was at the end of the war.

Wherever he went, he took his journal. It would be a remarkable document of the Civil War no matter where kept or by whom, if only for its outstanding literacy and style. But in the Confederate Army of Tennessee, it was truly exceptional. More important than the way it is written, however, is what it reveals about little-known episodes such as the mutinies in the Orphan Brigade. Its overall portrait of soldier life in a Western army is among the best we have. Moreover, Jackman's eyewitness accounts of events such as the famous snowball battle of 1864, the revival movement of the army, or the relative abundance of foodstuffs in some parts of Georgia even *after* Sherman had passed, will have long-lived importance to historians.

Interestingly, Jackman documented the writing of his diary. That is to say, he made note of when he kept daily entries and when he wrote from memory, making it much easier for a reader to determine what may be on-the-spot reporting and what benefits from hindsight. He kept no journal at all until March 30, 1862. About April 4, as the Battle of Shiloh became imminent, he stopped writing. Then, on the twelfth, the wrote the entries for April 4–12. From October 3–14 and October 27–December 5, 1862, he stopped daily entries again, writing them from memory when he recommenced. Jackman let the journal lapse again from January 6–April 23, 1863, filling in the blank days later from recollection. June 6–July 1, November 22–29, and the early days of December 1863 were also written afterward from memory. Then came his wounding on June 14, 1864, and Jackman did not write in his journal for three months, until September 23. From then until March 19, 1865, he was a diligent diarist, later adding his account of the final few weeks before his parole on May 6, 1865.

At first, apparently, Jackman made his daily entries in a notebook, but by December 1863 he had filled it. Subsequently, he made a journal out of old quartermaster forms on December 13, and he used that until March 19, 1865. When on campaign, he often made notes on whatever scraps of paper were readily at hand, then later copied them into his ersatz journal. Finally, the narrative from March 19– May 30, 1865, Jackman wrote from memory at some early subsequent date, most likely upon his return home to Kentucky. During those April weeks in Washington, Georgia, however, he transcribed into a new book all his notes from previous books, wrote from memory the first six months of his war service prior to Shiloh, and filled in some of the other blank spaces, "adding a little, occasionally, to be more explicit."

Consequently, what we have in the surviving Jackman journal is a wartime transcript, edited in the spring of 1865, incorporating contemporaneous notes and entries with some later wartime additions. Careful study reveals some entries that show hindsight, as with October 23, 1863, for instance, but the transcript as a whole is almost certainly the copy made by Jackman in 1865 and not subsequently altered or edited. For one thing, at the outset he writes that "nearly four years have passed" since he went off to war, clearly dating this part of the journal as no later than late 1865 in origin, thus agreeing with his note that he wrote the first six months from memory in April 1865. Also, the surviving journal has pasted into it copies of articles that Jackman published in the Memphis *Appeal* during the war, in their proper chronological location, almost certainly done in the spring of 1865. Throughout the journal, Jackman refers to most of his friends and associates only by initials or nicknames, whereas in any postwar transcription intended for reading by others, he would more likely have written out names completely. Furthermore, the final seventy-five pages of the journal following Jackman's last entry are filled with postwar newspaper clippings relating to the Orphan Brigade. They date from 1866 to 1908 or later, yet are not pasted in in any sort of chronological order, as would naturally be expected if the journal were a postwar transcription, made after many of the clippings were already in hand. The fact that the clippings are put in so randomly argues instead that the journal is 1865 in date and that Jackman filled the empty back pages with clippings as he found them in the years that followed.

Most persuasive of all, however, is the evidence of Ed Porter Thompson. In his *History of the First Kentucky Brigade*, published in 1868, he states on page 26 that "Mr. Jackman . . . generously laid his journal and other material before us, and otherwise assisted in our search for facts." On pages 121 and 122 of that book, Thompson quotes extensively from the July 15, 1862, entry in Jackman's journal, and his quote matches that entry in the surviving journal almost verbatim. This means that by 1867 at the latest—given a minimum of a year's press time for Thompson's book, including editing and so forth—Jackman's journal was in the form that it now survives.

Considering all this, there is no basis for supposing that Jackman's journal is not in fact a wartime work; the only hindsight from which any entries may benefit is relatively immediate wartime hindsight, thus making it all the more valuable and certainly more reliable than Green's and others' recollections many years after the fact. The journal itself is now a part of the collections of the Library of Congress, which purchased it in 1931 from an unspecified owner. It is entirely in Jackman's neat, small hand, including a few maps that he drew into the pages where appropriate. The several score clippings that occupy the back of the book almost all relate to the brigade. Many are articles written by Jackman himself, including a series done for the Louisville *Journal* in the late 1860's, and are based upon his wartime experience as related in the journal.

One of the enduring mysteries about Jackman's outfit is exactly how and when the name Orphan Brigade originated. For years it was assumed to be strictly a postwar appellation. The earliest known printed use of the term appeared in Thompson's 1868 brigade history, hidden away in a biographical sketch of Colonel Joseph Nuckols, and passed almost without notice.[7] In fact, Thompson's book makes an important point of the devotion of the men to their official name as the First Kentucky Brigade, mentioning also the sometime tendency to call themselves the "Old Brigade." In an 1868 review of the book pasted into Jackman's journal, the reviewer refers only once to the "Orphan Brigade."

Jackman uses the term three times in his journal, however. On May 30, 1862, he notes that "the 'orphans' are always cheerful." On

---

7. Ed Porter Thompson, *History of the First Kentucky Brigade* (Cincinnati: Caxton, 1868), p. 386.

December 13, 1862, he states that President Jefferson Davis, reviewing the Army of Tennessee, was "well pleased with the 'orphans'."
And finally, on July 8, 1863, he writes that news of the fall of Vicksburg "did not seem to affect the 'orphans' much." The December
1862 reference is almost certainly written not on that date but later.
The other two entries, however, may be as originally noted in his
journal. In any case, all three are within the portion of the journal
that Jackman transcribed at Washington, Georgia, in April 1865, and
thus are evidence for the first time that the term Orphan Brigade
was actually in use *during* the war, though it did not take general
hold on veterans until nearly twenty years later.[8] As for where the
name came from, Jackman, now the earliest known user of the term,
agrees with the reference in Thompson's 1868 book and later recollections by others. He said in an 1895 speech that the Kentuckians'
longtime commander General John C. Breckinridge gave them the
name at Stones River, after they were shattered in a futile assault and
their commander General Roger Hanson was killed. The brigade lost
one commander after another, including Breckinridge, who, said
Jackman, "always referred to them as his 'orphans'."[9]

If Jackman finished the final few weeks of his journal after he returned home to Kentucky, he did not spend too much time on it, for
he almost immediately set about making his future. As soon as his
health allowed, he went to Russellville to study law under Colonel
John W. Caldwell, formerly commander of the 9th Kentucky, and in
1869 Jackman was admitted to the state bar. Two years later he
moved to Louisville, and there he stayed for the rest of his life,
building a substantial chancery practice and winning for a time an
appointment as United States register in bankruptcy for the Louisville district.[10]

While building a secure law practice, Jackman never forgot his war
service or his comrades, or lost his literary bent. He was an active
participant at the Orphan Brigade reunions that began in 1881 and
continued well into the next century. He frequently wrote articles for
the Louisville press on Civil War topics, usually relating to his old
brigade. And in 1882 he and four others commenced publication of
the *Southern Bivouac*, sponsored by the Southern Historical Association of Louisville, of which Jackman was treasurer. The *Bivouac*, as

---

8. For a fuller discussion on the sobriquet, see Davis, p. 270.
9. Clipping in the Jackman journal, p. 204.
10. Johnston, p. 405; Levin, p. 303.

it was known, lasted only five years, three of them with Jackman as manager and contributor, but it proved to be one of the best of the veterans' publications devoted to the Confederacy, and today, like original sources dealing with the Orphan Brigade, it is one of the hardest to find.

John S. Jackman died in Louisville on December 21, 1912, and lies there today in Cave Hill Cemetery under a simple Confederate veteran's headstone, an unpretentious monument to an unpretentious yet remarkable young man. More important than any monument he might have left behind is the priceless document he gave to posterity. Indeed, so well written is the journal that it has required little editing. Jackman misspelled only a handful of words, and of those, only the ones for which the meaning might be obscure have been corrected by inserting in brackets the proper letters or words. His punctuation was idiomatic, with extensive use of dashes, hyphens, and commas. These, too, have been left as written, since they do not obscure his meaning. In short, with few exceptions the journal is exactly as Jackman finished it in 1865.

Scores of individuals are mentioned in the text, most often merely by initials. Thanks to the extensive biographical section of Thompson's two books on the brigade, most of the men Jackman mentions can be identified. A full identification is provided in a footnote the first time such a name appears, and it is not noted again afterward unless the possibility of confusion with someone else of the same initials could arise, or a substantial portion of time has elapsed since the last mention of that individual. Where there is an uncertainty about an identity, or if more than one person could fit the initials, then no notation or possible identification has been made. There are some names of persons and places that Jackman repeatedly misspells. Rather than correct each instance, the first usage only has been corrected, and thereafter Jackman's spelling is retained without comment unless some confusion might arise. If Jackman makes a substantive error or misstatement, of which there are a few, the correction has been made in a footnote. Also, examples of obvious after-the-fact or hindsight comments and conclusions have been noted. Finally, where contemporary slang or colloquialisms are used, they have been defined in footnotes where possible.

Jackman himself added a few footnotes by means of asterisks. All appear to be later additions to his text as he learned more about an event, but in no case do they appear to be based upon information he could not have obtained during the war, especially by the time of his last transcription of the journal in the spring of 1865. These notes have been left as written, essentially showing Jackman's editing of his own diary.

Several people have provided assistance with the editing of the Jackman journal. To the Library of Congress, ever the friend of historians, go thanks for making the document available for publication. To Dennis Byrne of Fairfax, Virginia, go the heartfelt thanks of an old friend for his help in copying difficult portions of the original that defied modern photocopiers. Frank Rankin of Louisville provided information on Jackman's death and burial, and James Klotter of the Kentucky Historical Society helped track down details on his postwar life and career. I. Beverly Lake of Wake Forest, North Carolina, generously made available the diary and papers of his ancestor Colonel John W. Caldwell, including the photograph of the flag of the 9th Kentucky that Jackman so proudly followed. And Diana L. Sacks of Harrisburg, Pennsylvania, bravely undertook to prepare a typewritten transcription of the bulk of the journal.

Thanks go to all of them. But most of all, thanks to young Johnny Jackman for answering the call of youth, for going off to seek adventure, for finding it, and for living through it all to tell us his story.

•1•

Out to Seek Adventures: The Kentucky Regiments Go South

Young John Jackman was only one of thousands of Kentucky men who found themselves lured to the cause of the South in 1861. Indeed, many had "gone South" before him, as the Kentucky regiments actually began formation across the line at Camp Boone, Tennessee, in July. The 2d Kentucky Infantry organized on July 13, followed by the 3d a few days later. On August 30 the 4th Kentucky was mustered in, and about the same time a battery of artillery from the Bluegrass State joined the regiments. In September Kentucky abandoned its stance of neutrality between Union and Confederacy, and forces from both sides moved into the state in the hope of taking it for their own. The Confederates, including the Kentucky regiments, moved to Bowling Green, and here young Jackman's regiment, the 5th Kentucky, was formed in October. Unbeknownst at the time, to its colonel, Thomas Hunt, another Kentucky regiment was forming in the eastern part of the state. The eastern regiment completed its organization first and was officially designated the 5th Kentucky by the Richmond war department. More than a year later, Hunt's regiment would finally be redesignated the 9th Infantry. Finally, on November 19, 1861, the 6th Kentucky organized. Together with the cavalry company of Captain John Hunt Morgan and the 1st Kentucky Cavalry of Colonel Ben Hardin Helm, the infantry regiments made up the First Kentucky Brigade.

The brigade organization would fluctuate in the years ahead, the cavalry units being soon taken away, but events began to move so quickly that there was little time for concern about the future. On November 16 a new commander took the brigade: Brigadier General John C. Breckinridge, a man whose career would be linked with that of his Kentuckians for the next two years of the war and forever into posterity. The next month portions of the brigade made their first movement, the Merry Oaks march. It was a false alarm but a hard tramp nevertheless for new soldiers. Then in January 1862 the 2d Kentucky and the Kentucky battery were sent to help defend Fort Donelson in Tennessee, where they surrendered the following month. Even before the sad news of the loss reached the men, the balance of the brigade joined the rest of the Confederates at Bowling Green in the evacuation of their encampments. They gave up Kentucky to the enemy—only for the moment, they hoped—and marched south through Tennessee and into Mississippi to strike their first blow.

Journal

The first six months of my "soldier life" I let pass without making notes of any kind. To make my Journal more complete, I shall write up that period from memory. I shall use no dates but those positively known to be correct.

(1861) Sept. 26th—Late in the afternoon left home with the intention of making my way to Green River, where the advance of the Confederate army was then encamped. My mind was made up to undertake this journey almost instantly. On the evening mentioned I walked down to the Depot, about car-time, to get the daily papers, and as I was passing in, W. S.[1] said to me, "Let us go to Bloomfield to-night, and join the party going through to Dixie!" or something to

---

1. William Stoner. Thompson, p. 823.

that effect. I had scarcely thought of such a thing before; but in an instant my mind was made up, and I answered, "All right." I immediately returned home and put on a heavy suit of cloths, and tried to slip off from the folks, but they divined my purpose. I told them I would only be gone a few days—that I was going to see Bro. Jo[2] and would be back. (My mind was not fully made up to join the army, when I left home—I was not satisfied my health would permit me). Taking nothing with me but a traveling shawl, I mounted and joined W. S. at his home. We were soon on the road, two modern Don Quixotes starting out to seek adventures.

There were then rendezvousing at camp "Charity"—so called because the people furnished us rations while there encamped—several companies from different counties, and among them was one from Bardstown, the "Nelson Grays."[3] To this company we purposed to attach ourselves during the trip, under temporary organization.

Though nearly four years have passed, the incidents of the journey to camp "Charity," and my first experience as a soldier, are still fresh in memory. The stirring scenes through which I have passed in nearly four years of warfare, have not dimmed from memory the most trifling occurrence.

There were several recruits from Samuel's Depot neighborhood going to Camp "Charity" that night, and arrangements had been made for all to meet at Mr. P.'s. W. S. and I took supper there. Shortly after dark we were ready, and my brother Don Quixote took leave of his Dulcinea. We rode off in high spirits. A short distance from P.'s, our party was augmented by three more boys. For fear of being molested by the home guards,[4] we went on by-roads, leaving Bardstown on our right. The night was beautiful. Nearly a full moon gave us light. Just before coming out on the main Bloomfield road, beyond Bardstown, "Capt." G.[5] and I rode forward as a reconnoitering party, to see that the road was clear. Finding all clear, we signaled the troop on, and met with no further delay until near camp. Then, we were riding along in high glee, and were suddenly chal-

2. Joseph Jackman, Company C, 2d Kentucky Infantry. Thompson, p. 567.

3. The Nelson Grays later became a part of Company B, 5th (9th) Kentucky.

4. The Home Guard was formed in Kentucky to rival the pro-Southern State Guard, and consisted of Unionists from throughout the state. In many towns, Home Guard and State Guard companies mustered and paraded on the same field. Davis, pp. 9–10.

5. "Capt. G." is probably John Gates, Company B, 5th (9th) Kentucky. Thompson, p. 819.

lenged "Who comes there?" Silence came over our party immediately, and "Capt." G., who was at the head, answered promptly, "Recruits for the Rebel army." We were then commanded to halt, and a picket came forward to inspect. This was something novel to me—this was soldiering in reality. As the picket advanced, I caught a glimpse of his polished bayonet as it gleamed in the moonlight. That was the first bayonet I had seen in actual use, to overturn the "best government the World ever saw." I shall never forget my feelings, at first beholding that polished steel glittering in the moon-beams.

After being satisfied that we were all right, the picket conducted us to the stand, and another one set out with us, to show us the way to camp. Being then midnight, and all the fires having burnt down, we were very close to the camp before we knew it. A sentinel on post challenged us, and I distinctly heard the clicking of his lock, as he drew the hammer back. I thought this extreme vigilence. After parlying sometime with the sentinel, who was green, we were taken in by Capt. W.,[6] afterward Lieut. Col., and conducted to the bivouac of his company. A fire was recruited, and we sat round chatting awhile with James H.,[7] and others hailing from about Samuel's who had preceded us the day before. Being weary, I soon rolled myself up in my shawl, and tumbled down under a large beech tree, to sleep. I lay a moment watching the "lamps of heaven" as they twinkled through the foliage of the old tree, my thoughts busy contemplating the *sublimeness* of soldiering—then I sank into a restless slumber.

Sept. 27th.—At daylight, woke with the rain pattering down in my face. I broiled a piece of fat bacon on the end of a stick, and with a fragment of corn-bread, made my breakfast. I then looked around to see what I could see. Camp "Charity" I found to be three miles from Bloomfield, and on no very public road. There was an old log church in the centre of the bivouac, which was used for an arsenal and commissary depot.[8] The men, (who were mostly

---

6. John C. Wickliffe was elected captain of Company B, 5th (9th) Kentucky, on October 2, 1861, and eventually became lieutenant colonel of the regiment. Thompson, pp. 447–50.

7. James Hunter, commissary of Company B. Thompson, p. 820.

8. Rendezvous camps were established at several points in Kentucky, and Camp Charity became a gathering point for many small bands of young men from north central Kentucky. By virtue of his commission as captain in the State Guard, John Hunt Morgan assumed informal command. Davis, p. 30.

dressed in gay uniforms,) were sheltered by rude arbors made of tree-branches. There were then between two and three hundred men in camp. The "Lexington Rifles," a company commanded by Capt. John H. Morgan, afterwards a noted cavalry General in the Confederate service, was present. Morgan was commander-in-chief of the forces.[9]

At 9 a.m., was placed on guard, and for the first time "buckled on my armor." How proud I felt as I paced to and fro on my beat, with a long sabre bayonet on my gun, which glittered not a little in the sun-beams. There was no rain after daylight, and the sun came out bright and clear. Had a good dinner. James H., who was in the commissary department, fed me on pies and such things. That was the best commissariat we ever had. That night, until the moon came up, was black as Erebus, and my beat was back of the camp, in a dense wood. I could only "step on the track." I was delighted at hearing my brother sentinels challenging and calling for the corporal. They generally used their lungs pretty freely, and I imagined they could be heard for miles. I longed for an opportunity to try my lungs, *a la militaire;* but I had almost despaired of finding a pretext, when one suddenly offered. The hour was after midnight, and all quiet as death. I heard two fellows coming to the spring, which was just inside my beat. I walked to one extremity and kept still, hoping they would miss their way and wander over. Sure enough they did. They soon found out their mistake and started again for the spring, but I halted them "instanter." They commenced begging me to let them in, but I pompously told them *my duty* kept me from letting any one pass my post, unless first giving the countersign, which they did not have. The next moment "corporal of the guard, post no. 8," was bawled out by me in my best military manner. It was passed from sentinel to sentinel to my entire satisfaction. Even the owls stopped hooting, either through respect, or being terror-stricken. Presently I heard the corporal coming, tumbling over logs and swearing true trooper style. The "corp" let the water-hunters in, and I was left to pace my beat, "solitary and alone." Two years after, I met the corporal—then a lieutenant—at

---

9. John Hunt Morgan would be closely associated with the 1st Kentucky Brigade in its early months, later commanding a squadron of cavalry attached to the brigade until the spring of 1862, after which he went on to become a general and one of the Confederacy's most dashing raiders.

Dalton, Ga., and I told him how I played off on him—he laughed heartily.

Sept. 28th.—At 2 o'clock P.M. our little army took up its line of march for Green River. We had been recruited to upwards of 400— about equally divided, foot and horse. Our departure was amid tears of the gentler sex, who were present to bid relatives farewell. The column moved off, nearly all joining in singing a war-song. Many who then marched away with bouyant step, were doomed never to return. They found graves far from home—far from kindred!

We presented quite a formidable appearance—we "night hunters." All well armed, and all, save those who had old muskets, had forty rounds of ammunition. Our course lay in four miles of Bardstown, where we had learned a force had been sent to intercept us. Morgan rode at the head of the column unperturbed. We passed all the roads without interruption. Night overtook us just beyond the Springfield pike, and was very dark. Our course led mostly through the woods, and often we followed by-pathes. The infantry marched in front, in two ranks, and the cavalry brought up the rear. Our wagon train consisted of a small spring-wagon, used for hauling ordnance, etc., and a buggy, in which was the Rev. Dr. Ford and his wife. It has always been a mystery how our "train" got over such a rough road. There was also a trader along, with a small drove of mules. A lantern was carried at the head of the column, which those in the rear could occasionally see, as we wended our way through the dark woods. The infantry were "ferried over" the Beech Fork mounted behind the cavalry. When over, all the cavalry were requested to dismount and let the infantry ride awhile, but many refused to dismount. In the confusion, part of us took the wrong road. We got righted at last, after much trouble, and moved on rapidly to overtake the advance. I had to help James H. along. (Someone had promised to give him a horse if he would ride it. He mounted exultingly, but was barely seated when the horse ran off with him, and threw him against a tree, hurting him so he could scarcely walk.) Camp-fires were seen ahead of us, and the report got started that the enemy was in front. Capt. M. swore he would not lead his men into action unless there was an equal distribution of cartridges! Some even leveled their guns to shoot in direction of the fires. I now saw what I had considered a body of *veteran* troop[s] turned into a mob. I knew that if we did meet with any resistance—I was certain the enemy was not encamped there—such conduct as was then exhibited would cause us to "go up."[10] James H. and I thought seriously of forsaking the crowd and shifting for ourselves. The fires had been kindled by those in advance, who were waiting for us to come up.

[Sept.] 29th.—At daylight we crossed the Lebanon Branch Railroad. After crossing a long rocky hill, we stopped on the side of a creek to breakfast. I had walked 40 miles without hardly resting, carrying my gun and 40 rounds—also some articles of clothing. My breakfast was a piece of beef, broiled on the end of a stick, without salt. After resting about an hour we pushed on. I thought to ride awhile, but we had scarcely got on the road before a report came that the enemy was in front. I took my place in the company on foot. We waded a deep creek without breaking ranks—it would not have been *soldierly* to have done otherwise—and my boots drew to my feet so, when in the sun, that I could not walk. I then rode until we got to the top of Muldraugh's Hill. The day was beautiful, and the scenery on the road was often picturesque. Sometimes our road led under rocky steeps, where we could have been destroyed by a handful of men with ease. I was too tired to admire the scenery much. After dismounting on top of the Hill, I had not crippled far, before the infantry was ordered to mount behind the cavalry. It fell to my lot to be mounted behind a very large man on a very small horse. Just before coming out on the Elizabethtown pike, a fight seemed imminent, and the big man on the little horse put me down to shift for myself. I had not gone far, however, when a Don Quixotic looking individual took me up. We passed out on the pike without molestation. Our march was continued until long after dark. I was so sleepy I could scarcely sit on the horse. I reeled about so, my "Don" often threatened to put me down. At last we got to "Sandy-Hollow," where we camped. I tumbled off the horse, down by a big oak tree, not even taking time to wrap up in my shawl and went to sleep. It was broad daylight when I awoke. Hill[11] lay down near me across some rails that were on fire, and he slept so soundly that his coat was burned off without breaking his slumbers.

Sept. 30th.—We moved out early. I mounted N. O.'s[12] horse. Had not proceeded far, when a drum commenced to rattle out in the bushes, and firing of small arms commenced in front. I thou't the ball

---

10. "Go up" was short for "go up the spout," soldiers' slang for something gone wrong, the Civil War equivalent of World War II's "snafu."

11. Joseph S. Hill, Company B, 5th (9th) Kentucky. Thompson, p. 820.

12. Noel Overall, Company B, 5th (9th) Kentucky. Thompson, p. 822.

had opened, and unslung my gun. The drum was beat by a body of
home-guards—and they also soon "beat a retreat" further into the
woods—and the firing in front came from the advance, killing turkeys for breakfast. At a little town, just before we left the pike, the
United States flag was floating quietly on the breeze, at the top of a
high poll. It was not molested by us. We halted at noon to rest, not
to dine, for we had nothing to eat. That afternoon I could not walk,
and our captain mounted me on his horse. At last we came to the top
of a high range of hills, where we could survey the Green River valley. Far away we could see the river threading its way among the
blue hills; and looking more narrowly, could see the tents of the Confederates dotting the valley. The day was beautiful—such as we generally have during the indian-summer. The smoke from the camps
hazed the landscape, giving additional beauty. We had yet to travel
several miles, and it was dark when we arrived at the camp of the 2d
Ky.,[13] which was at the south end of the railroad bridge. We were
welcomed by music and the firing of cannon. Being on horseback, I
went with the balance of the cavalry to a cavalry camp close by. I was
so exhausted from travel, that I could not dismount, and was taken
from my horse and placed in the tent of H. who gave me a pint of
coffee and a piece of camp-baked bread. I slept well that night. This
was the first time I ever slept in a tent.

Oct. 1st.—We commenced camp-life—learning how to cook, pitch
tents, drill etc., etc. I could not walk about much, my feet were so
sore. Afterwards all the nails came off my toes. Saw my brother Jo
and several old acquaintances of the 2d. I had expected to see the
soldiers better clad than I found them—they were very ragged and
dirty. Our camp was a short distance from the 2d Reg't.

Oct. 2d.—The company held a council of war in the morning, and
resolved to go into the service under old organization. That evening
we fell in and marched to the headquarters of the 2d Ky., where we
were sworn into the service of the Confederate States by Maj.
Hewitt.[14] We were to serve for three years, or during the war. When
we started back, the soldiers standing about who then considered

---

13. The 2d Kentucky was the first organized of the regiments that formed the 1st
Kentucky Brigade, and was stationed at Bowling Green to recruit men for the succeeding regiments. Davis, p. 27.

14. Major James W. Hewitt, 2d Kentucky Infantry, would eventually rise to lieutenant colonel. He was killed at Chickamauga on September 20, 1863. Thompson, pp.
439–40.

•

themselves veterans, but who had, in fact, seen no service, commenced bawling out: "Sold to the Dutch"—"Sold to the Dutch!" in order to make us feel bad.[15]

Just before sun-down the company fell in under arms and we marched out beyond Mumfordsville to do picket duty. There was a company of the *veterans* with us. They guarded the dirt road—we the pike. Our base, though, was at the same place, in an old orchard near town. That night one of our boys, while out on vidette, shot at an old sow, thinking her an enemy—one of the "vets" shot at a *rock* in the road, thinking it a sneaking foe. Just before daylight, my time came to go on vidette, and I had not been on post long before I heard many hoofs clattering on the pike, advancing with the rattling of sabres, and loud talk. My hair at first went on end, but soon the horsemen were close up, and I could see through the gray light of morning, their still grayer uniforms. They were scouts returning to camp.

Oct. 3d.—Lying around all day without rations. Not relieved until after dark. When we got back to our quarters, we found the 2d had moved back to Rowlett's station, two or three miles from the river. The old gentlemen who had come out with us, and had remained in camp, cooked supper for us. We had great piles of straw in our tents, and I slept soundly.

Oct. 4th.—At noon marched back to Rowlett's. When our baggage came down on the rail road, we went to work and pitched our tents within the lines of the 2d Ky. We were then ordered to strike them, and move across the rail road. We again got in the wrong place, and had to move. At last the Citizen Guards from Louisville,[16] and our company, pitched tents on a grassy lawn, on the roadside, and ceased our labors.

Oct. 5th.—In the evening the two companies took the train for Bowling Green, and arrived there just after dark. When we saw the camp-fires in the suburbs, all said the world was there encamped.[17]

---

15. "Sold to the Dutch" was a frequent jibe shouted at new recruits, hinting that they were about to be ground up in battle fighting foreign-born enlistees in Union regiments.

16. The Citizen Guards from Louisville later joined with Jackman's small group to make up part of Company B, 5th (9th) Kentucky. Kirwan, p. 11.

17. General Albert Sidney Johnston, appointed overall confederate commander between the Alleghenies and the Mississippi, was building his Army of Central Kentucky in and around Bowling Green, hoping to use it to take and hold all of Kentucky up to the Ohio River.

We knew little about armies then. The two companies immediately
marched out 2 miles N.W. from town, where two other companies
purposed to be in the same regiment, were encamped. They had a
guard on, and *Leander Washington Applegate* was corporal of said
guard.[18] Leander talked wonderfully through his nose, and offered us
no little amusement. I afterwards found him to be a "bully fellow."
He at last let us in, and we pitched tents, dark as it was. We had no
straw, and I came near freezing, in-as-much as one of the boys wound
my shawl around himself, leaving me on the ground without covering. When I awoke my teeth were chattering. I then placed my
friend in a freezing condition by unwinding him.

The next day we established Camp Warren on the spot. Colonel
H.[19] came out, and commenced organizing the reg't. There were already four companies in camp—a company from about Owensboro',
the Citizen Guards, the "Portland Roughs," from Portland, and our
company.[20] A camp guard was established, and drilling commenced.
We soon after got a kettle-drum, which was rattled to perfection by
Mon., or Prof. Francois Gevers.[21] While here, we had good rations
issued, and learned how to cook them. After being in camp a week
or so, I was detailed to work on a bake-oven in town, and the first
day lost my shawl. A day or two afterwards the regiment moved
nearer town, to camp "Dismal." The next day the rain pourd down
incessantly. My brother Don Quixote[22] was on police, pulling up
the tall rag-weeds about camp. Once he came to the tent, in which
we had built a fire, and of course had plenty of smoke. "Bro. Don"
was not in a good humor, and I shall not attempt to say, what he said
on that occasion. That night I went to a Hotel; but I had been used
to sleeping on the ground, and could not sleep in a good bed—I
rested badly.

The next morning we took train for Russellville, but did not leave
Bowling Green until nearly night. When we got to R——, it was
dark as pitch, and rain pouring down in torrents. We got off the cars

---

18. Leander W. Applegate, Company H, 5th (9th) Kentucky. Thompson, p. 848.
See "Taps," *Southern Bivouac*, I (February 1883), pp. 271–72, for a characteristic Applegate story.

19. Colonel Thomas H. Hunt recruited and commanded the 5th (9th) Kentucky
from the outset until his resignation on April 22, 1863. Thompson, pp. 430–32.

20. Soon to form Company B and other companies of the 5th (9th) Kentucky.

21. Francis A. Gervers, Company B, 5th (9th) Kentucky, was French by birth. Thompson, p. 819.

22. William Stoner.

and marched up to the Court House, where we quartered for the night.

The following day a camping ground was selected near town, on the side of the rail road, and we went regularly into camp. Here three more companies joined us—two made up in Logan and Todd counties, and one from Ohio county.[23]

While at camp "Magruder,"[24] the people treated us well. Many ladies visited our camp, and often brought us baskets of nice provisions. Here we first drilled in battalion, our regiment being of pretty good size. Our drums were increased to at least a dozen, small and great, and the field band at Reville had to march (drumming) through all the streets. The noise was sufficient to wake the Seven Sleepers.

Camped at Russellville until the latter part of November, when we moved by rail to Bowling Green. Many ladies were present at our departure, to bid relatives farewell, which was done amid much weeping on the part of the ladies.

We went into camp (Price)[25] in the suburbs of town. Here we were regularly mustered into the service and drew our first uniforms.[26]

About the 1st of December I took the camp fever, and was sent to regimental hospital in town. Our regiment had two very nice buildings for that purpose. I was pretty sick for awhile. The day after Christmas, I was sent in charge of a party of convalescents to Camp "Recovery," which was at some winter quarters, four or five miles from town, on the Nashville pike. The cabins had been put up by part of the brigade and left. There were eight or ten of us, and we had a cabin all to ourselves—but no cooking utensiles. The first night, at a late hour, the pickets commenced firing on the road and we were all turned out under arms. Capt. S.,[27] commander, gave me

---

23. Later Companies A, C, and G, 5th (9th) Kentucky.

24. Probably so named after Brigadier General John B. Magruder, whose small command won the war's first land battle the previous June at Big Bethel, Virginia.

25. Named after Major General Sterling Price, victor in the battle of Wilson's Creek the past August, in Missouri.

26. This is the point at which the confusion of two 5th Kentucky Infantries commences. Hunt completed organization of his regiment, mustering it into service, about the end of November 1861. However, another Kentucky regiment had completed its organization and mustered in on November 14, predating Hunt by a few days. Both were to be known as the 5th Kentucky until October 1862, when Hunt's regiment was redesignated the 9th Kentucky, and it is thus referred to hereinafter. Thompson, p. 45.

27. Probably Assistant Surgeon Alfred Smith, 9th Kentucky. Thompson, p. 622.

charge of thirty or forty men, and ordered me to defend the part of camp most exposed to attack. I divided my ammunition, which made one round to the man—some of the cartridges would't fit—and marched to the position assigned me. We waited patiently for the enemy to appear. While changing my front a little, making consider- able noise, someone out on the field challenged us. We asked who it was but received an evasive answer. We heard several guns cocked out in front. We made ready. But instead of firing, we commenced questioning, and I found the "army" opposing us was a scout sent out to reconnoiter, and now returning with the report that no enemy could be found. We disbanded and went to bed.

The next day walked to Bowling Green. Felt strong.

The following day applied to go to my command, and walked to town in time for the train. Soon ran up to Oakland, 12 miles, and there found the regiment encamped. Was glad to be with the boys again. The brigade, commanded by Brig. Gen'l Breckinridge,[28] had just returned from what they always termed the "Merry Oaks march." They represented it as a very hard march—disagreeable— and since, have always spoken of that, as being one of their *hard* times.[29]

I believe the next day we were mustered for pay.[30] Then, I saw Gen'l John C. Breckinridge for the first time—he inspected us. Our regiment was then considerably reduced from sickness. Here Billie S——r[31] first complained of sickness.

January 1st, 1862, we moved camp to "Clear-Water," two or three miles off the railroad, and near the pike. We were near a church which was used as regt'l hosp'tl. No other troops were camped near us. The first thing I did after the tent was pitched, was adding a sod chimney, which answered us a good purpose, while there encamped. We had a little A tent, and seven in the mess—two being very large men. There was a great deal of rain fell, and about camp was very

---

28. John C. Breckinridge of Kentucky.

29. On December 22 Breckinridge led the brigade on a ten-mile march from Bowl- ing Green, getting only as far as Merry Oaks before the snow and ice halted the com- mand. Learning the next morning that a rumored threat from the enemy in that direction was only imaginary, he led the men back in a grueling trek that, being their first hard march, the men never forgot. Davis, p. 60.

30. Jackman was paid on January 1, 1862. John S. Jackman Compiled Service Record, Record Group 109, National Archives, Washington, D.C. (hereinafter cited as Jackman, Service Record).

31. William Stoner. Thompson, p. 823.

muddy. The colonel had old tan-bark hauled to pave the streets, and had it piled on all the beats. Some times, on a dark night, a sentinel could not keep on the little ridge of bark, and would get off into mud knee deep.

We had been in camp but a few days when Billie S——r was sent to the hospital with the typhoid fever, and soon after died. A week or two afterward three others, of the mess, were sent off—"Bro. Don" N. O. and "Capt." G.[32]—Billie A., G. P.[33] and myself, were all that remained. Four of the company died in hospital, while encamped at "Clear-Water," and retreating, left N. O. at Gallatin, Tenn., who died.

I had not been well since my return to the regiment, and about the middle of February was sent to the regimental hospital, still being kept up in Bowling-Green. There had been a great deal of sickness in camp. All of one company from Texas,[34] which had been attached to our regiment, were sent to the hospital, save one little boy—a drummer. I found "Bro. Don" and N. O. very sick, and staying at a private house in town. Capt. G. (unwell) was giving them attention. I also went to see Capt. W.,[35] who was very sick, at a private house.

The next day the brigade passed through marching towards Nashville. Dr. P.[36] broke up the regimental hospital, and accompanied the regiment. We were all transferred to another hospital near the Depot, to be shipped on the cars. That evening "Bro. Don" and N. O. were moved to the same place. And a hard place it was. Just before daylight the next morning, a fire broke out on main street on the public square, and caused a great deal of confusion. Walls were battered down by using artillery, to stop the spreading flames.

That morning, after daylight, all the sick were moved to the Depot to be loaded on the cars. I hope never to witness another such scene as was presented there that day. Men at the lowest stage of sickness were not half attended, and were thrown around like the commonest freight. Many died from want of attention. There was no official present to direct the removal of the sick—every body for himself.

32. Noel Overall and John Gates, Company B, 9th Kentucky. Thompson, pp. 819, 822. "Bro. Don" cannot be identified.
33. William Ambrose and George Pash, Company B, 9th Kentucky. Thompson, pp. 816, 822.
34. The Texans formed part of Company H, 9th Kentucky. Thompson, pp. 848–57.
35. Captain John C. Wickliffe.
36. Dr. John E. Pendleton, surgeon of the 9th Kentucky. Thompson, p. 807.

Capt. G. and myself were able to walk about, and we had to give all
of our attention to the two boys named; also to another of the company very sick. They all had the typhoid fever. We got into a passenger car and it was noon before we moved off. Then all the troops had
left, and the Federal soldiers were near. About sundown we got to
Franklin. From that time until daylight the next morning, we were
on the road to Gallatin. The weather turned cold that night, and a
snow two or three inches deep fell. The train was so heavy, the engineer said, that he could not pull it. I believe he wanted it captured.
I did not sleep a moment that night. The car was crowded to overflowing with sick, and I had to stand up a great deal of the time. At
daylight we got to Gallatin, and Capt. G. and I went to a hotel and
got our breakfast. We brought the boys something to eat. All day
long the train was trying to make it over a grade running up from the
depot. In the evening, late, the engineer and fireman got drunk, and
were arrested by the military. Capt. G. took the three boys off the
train, and moved them to a private house. There N. O. died.[37]

I remained on the train, and at sun down a new engine was
hitched on, and we went flying to Nashville. I could scarcely walk to
the hosptl near by. There were several of us together, and all the
bunks being occupied, we had to sleep on the floor by the stove.
There were 250 sick men in that room, their bunks all arranged
in rows. A cold chill ran over me at seeing so many pale faces by
gas-light.

The next day looking in all the hospitals for brother Jo, but did not
find him. That morning or the next, I have forgotten which, the news
came of the fall of Fort Donelson, and the whole city was thrown into
consternation.[38] Excited crowds collected on the corners, and we
were harangued by prominent citizens. Commissary and Quartermaster depots were thrown open to the populace; citizens commenced packing up and moving off; & the hospital rats commenced
bundling up and "shoving out"—in fact there was great confusion.
The evening of the same day the startling news came, my regiment
passed through on the march, and I slung my knapsack; shouldred

---

37. Overall was left sick in Gallatin, Tennessee, where he died in February 1862.
Thompson, p. 822.

38. Fort Donelson fell to the Federals on February 16, 1862, and with it the 2d
Kentucky surrendered. Loss of the fort made the Confederate position at Bowling
Green untenable, forcing the abandonment of Kentucky.

my gun, and fell into ranks. I could scarcely walk though. We camped four or five miles from town that night.

The next day we marched four or five miles farther towards Murfreesboro', and camped. The weather looked so favorable that evening, we neglected to ditch our tent, and were well paid for our negligence. That night, at a late hour, a heavy rain-storm came up, and perfect rivers were running under us, from that 'till morning. Of course rested badly.

The following day, the rain pourd down incessently. We made a fire in our tent, and by night my eyes were nearly out from smoke. Here we received a lot of overcoats, hats and gloves—a present to the regiment, from the merchants of New Orleans.

The day after, our company wagon was sent to the city for clothing; but before it got back in the evening, the regiment had moved. I was left to help load in our baggage. We had to tumble the boxes off in the road, to make room for our camp equipage. After we were loaded, I took an axe, bursted some of the boxes, and heaped clothing on top of our load as long as it would stay—the balance was burned. We marched about 10 miles and bivouacked.

The next morning, the intermittent fever had a good hold on me, and I had to be hauled on a wagon all day. That evening we went into camp half a mile south of Murfreesboro'. Here "Capt." G. got with us.

The day following, raining hard all day long. I lay in the tent with a high fever. Dr. P. came to see me and gave me medicine. That evening Col. H. gave me a pass, approved by Genl Breckinridge, to go to a private house. I objected going to a hospital. I got into an ambulance to be taken to town; but it got stuck in the mud, and I slept in it all night.

Next morning "Capt." G. placed me in a large spring wagon, and we were nearly all day finding a place to stop. At last "Prof." Francois[39] took me to a family where he was staying. The accommodations were poor, but it was the best we could do. I had to sleep on the floor the first night. After that, though, had a bed provided. The "Pro." staid with me, and was very kind. I was out of my head a great deal—bad off. Dr. P. and S. visited me daily.

When the troops left, about a week after, I was still sick; but I had "Capt." G. to take me to the depot, and was placed in a passenger

---

39. Francis Gevers.

coach. I was again fated to be packed like a sardine in a sick car. Dr. V.,[40] of the 6th Ky., was aboard, and if it had not been for him, I don't believe I could have kept up. The train ran down as far as Tullahoma by dark, and laid over for daylight. All the next day we were running to Chattanooga. I was burning with fever all the time, and often I looked out the window at the clear mountain streams, dashing over the rocks, and wished to be bathing in them. The weather was cold then.

We were in the car-shed at Chattanooga until the next evening at 6 o'clock. I could get nothing which I could eat. Coffee was given me, but it made me sick. A. W.[41]—who belonged to the same company, was very kind to me. He afterwards died on [in] the hospital.

The night we were on the train for Atlanta was very disagreeable. The water gave out and I sat by a window and caught the rain in a cup, drop by drop, as it fell off the car. I was glad of its raining that night.

The train arrived at Atlanta about daylight, and we were taken to the old C[i]ty Hotel, which was being fitted up for a hospital. So many sick were being brought to the city, that they could be but poorly accommodated. We had to lie down on the hard floor. A doctor came to me just in the nick of time, and had mustard plasters put on my chest. I was in great pain.

The next morning I felt better, and A. W. got me some soup, which was the first nourishment I had taken for days. That day a gentleman from Louisville, Mr. S., came and took four of us, belonging to the same company, to the Washington Hall, a first class hotel. I commenced improving, and in two weeks could walk about the streets. I then reported to go to my command—which I afterwards regretted, for the exposure came near "fixing" me again. I went before I was entirely recovered.

About 30 of us were placed under the charge of a Lt. Whetstone,[42] and locked up in a car for Chattanooga. The commander of the post made us a little speech before he fastened us up, hoping we would be orderly, *keep on train, etc.* We left at 7 p.m., and arrived at C. about the same time the next morning. We got off the train, and I

40. Dr. John L. Vertrees, assistant surgeon of the 6th Kentucky. Thompson, p. 742.

41. A. M. Wayne, Company B, 9th Kentucky, died in August 1862. Thompson, p. 824.

42. Probably Lieutenant W. D. Whetstone, 21st Alabama Infantry. *Confederate Veteran*, XIX (September 1911), p. 433.

never again saw the Lt. He was such a "goober" I don't believe he knew which road to take. Here I spent the last money for breakfast— a piece of fat pork and a bit of corn bread. Left C. at 8 a.m., and arrived at Huntsville that afternoon. Lay over at H. until 2 the next morning, when we ran down to Decatur. I had nothing to buy my breakfast, and tried to trade my pocket knife to an old negro for a piece of ginger-bread, but we could't come to terms. I then went to a camp close by, and got my breakfast gratis. Sometime in the forenoon the train left for Corinth. I got into the same car with two soldiers from the 6th Ky., who had their wives along, which wives had a very large basket of provisions. I soon ingratiated myself with the ladies, and as a consequence, "lived high" the balance of the trip. The train got to Burnsville, Miss., late at night, and finding our brigade was encamped there, I got off. Some of the boys were in town on detail, and I stayed with them 'till morning. Early I went to camp, and found all the boys "*in status quo.*"

The brigade had marched all the way from Bowling-Green to Decatur, Ala., having been transported by rail from the latter place to Burnsville. I missed nearly all of this march, but I would rather have gone through it, then suffered as I did.

I have now written up to the time I commenced keeping notes. I shall now transcribe those notes, adding a little, occasionally, to be more explicit.

•2•

This Day Will Long Be
Remembered: Shiloh

*The taste of action that many of the Kentuckians so desired
finally came to them in two days of bloody battle at Shiloh on
April 6–7, 1862. None were prepared for what they encoun-
tered. Breckinridge had been promoted to corps command, so
the brigade was led into battle by Colonel Robert P. Trabue of
the 4th Kentucky. Under his command it was the fate of the
brigade to be involved in the very hottest of the fight on the
first day. In the area known ever after as the Hornets' Nest,
they performed admirably. The next day, when the Confederates retired from the field, it fell to the Kentucky brigade to
cover the retreat, an arduous and often dangerous post that
would become almost customary service for them.*

*The Confederates withdrew to Corinth, Mississippi, where
they were confronted by a slow and hesitating Federal pursuit,
and where, inexplicably, their army commander divided the
regiments of the brigade. The 4th and the 5th (later 9th) and
the battery were placed with two Alabama regiments in one brigade, while the 6th, the 3d, and the 7th Kentucky and another
Kentucky battery were added to yet another Alabama unit to
make a second brigade. They were still arguing over which was
entitled to be called the First Kentucky Brigade when the army
evacuated Corinth on May 28 and withdrew to Tupelo.*

March 30th. Being sunday morning, the boys are rubbing up for inspection to be at 2 o'clock P.M. Drill in camp. Am not well.

Evening. Heavy firing of artillery in the direction of the Tennessee. First hostile guns heard. The firing lasted some time, and made me feel "devilish," as the deep thunder came rolling over the hills. All on the *qui vive* to know the cause. The company ordered to be ready to march at 5, morning.

March 31st. The company, with two others from the regiment, marched at 5 a.m. Was not able to go. The cannonading yesterday was at East Port, on the Tenn. river. Was caused by our scouts firing into a Federal gun boat, which then shelled the shore.

Our camp is in a pine hill near Burnsville, Miss., which is a small village on the Memphis & Charlston R.R.

April 1st. Company came in at noon. Had been on a foraging expedition. Saw where the shelling took place. At 9 P.M. ordered to cook two days rations, and be ready to move at moment's notice.

April 2d. This season "Her Gentleness" seems tardy in robing old earth in a mantle of green. However she has commenced work. The forests are greening, and the flowers blooming. These remind me of happier days! All quiet in military line.

April 3d. Through the day drew and cooked up three days rations; and forty rounds issued to the man. After dark, the regiment was drawn up before the colonel's tent, and a battle order read.[1]

April 4th. Had reveille at 4, and marched at daylight. Nearly all the baggage was sent to Corinth by a direct road. We had to strike tents and load baggage in a pelting rain. Being weak and debilitated, and feeling like a stimulant, I picked up a bottle, in which I thought was whiskey, but upon turning it up and taking a "big horn," I found [it] to be alcohol and camphor mixed—medicine for the "Prof's" rheumatism. I thought the stuff would burn me up—it cut blood out of my throught [throat]. That tought me a lesson.

At the outset our road led through a swamp, where, in some places, the mud and water was knee deep every step. The rain continued to pour down all the four noon [forenoon]. I soon regretted

---

1. Colonel Hunt read army commander General Albert Sidney Johnston's battle order of April 3, 1862, addressed to "Soldiers of the Army of the Mississippi." It reminded the men that "the eyes of eight millions of people rest upon you." U.S. War Department, *War of the Rebellion: Official Records of the Union and Confederate Armies* (Washington: Government Printing Office, 1880–1901), series I, volume 10, part II, p. 389 (cited hereinafter as *O.R.*).

that I had started. For a time I kept up, but soon the column commenced creeping past me. While the troops would be resting, I would be walking to overtake them. About noon our road led over piny ridges, and the sun came out very hot. Once I stopped off on the side of the road at a spring, to rest. While resting, some soldier took my nice minnie rifle,[2] which I had left leaning against a tree, and left his old flint-lock in the place. I was vexed. When I got back on the road I found the division,[3] commanded by Gen'l Breckinridge, the only troops on that road, had all past, and the wagon train moving by. I gave up walking any farther, and got into our surgeon's wagon. At sundown, we passed through Farmington, 4 miles of Corinth. Night soon overtook us, and as the road often led over creeks, which were swampy, the train had to stop before coming up with the column. That night it rained and James H. and I slept in a wagon. I had a high fever that night.

April 5th. This morning, felt completely broken down. The wagon was so heavily loaded, and behind too, I had to try it afoot again—the train rolled past me, and I was left a complete straggler. A staff officer, in charge of the rear, ordered me back to Corinth, but as soon as he was gone, I kept ahead. The next house I came to I stopped. The lady gave me some milk and bread to eat. I felt so bad, I thought I would go no further. Soldiers were straggling along all day. That evening, there was some artillery firing towards Shiloh. Again had fever that night.

April 6th. This day will long be remembered. Soon after the sun had risen, the firing of artillery became so general, and the roar of musketry could be heard so distinctly, I knew the battle had commenced. I wished to be on the field, but was not able to walk so far. The gentleman with whom I was staying had his only remaining horse caught, which I mounted. When I bade "mine hostess" goodbye, she looked very "sorrowful"—which affected me not a little & I never knew why she took such an interest in me. The gentleman walked and kept up. Four miles brought us to Monterey, and just beyond, we met some of the wounded on foot with their arms and

---

2. Jackman is, of course, referring to the minié bullet for use with rifled firearms, named after its French inventor. Hunt's was the most ill-armed of the Kentucky regiments, and Jackman's weapon was probably one of the old-style rifled muskets known to have been in the regiment. Davis, p. 48.

3. In fact, Jackman and the Kentucky brigade were not part of a division but were joined with two other brigades to form the Reserve Corps of the army.

heads bound up in bloody bandages, & I felt then that I was getting in the vicinity of "warfare." Soon we met ambulances and wagons loaded with wounded, and I could hear the poor fellows groaning and shrieking, as they were being jolted over the rough road. Met a man on horseback with a stand of captured colors. We were now in proximity of the fighting, and we met crowds of men; some crippling along, wounded in the legs or about the body; others, no blood could be seen about their persons—yet all seemed bent on getting away. I now dismounted and started on foot. I never saw the gentleman afterwards, who had kindly brought me so far on the road. Being in so much excitement, I became stronger. I met a fellow dressed in a suit of "butter-nut" jeans, who was limping, but I don't believe was scratched. He asked me, in that whining way: "Has you'ns been in the fight yet?" I thought he meant some general, and asked my "brown" interrogator what troops General "Youens" commanded. He seemed astounded, and at last made me understand him. I told him "no," and went on. I afterwards got quite familiar with the "youens" and "weens" vernacular of "Brown Jeans."[4]

While passing a hospital on the roadside, I happened to see one of our company lying by a tent wounded. I went out to see him, and there found the brigade hospital established. There were heaps of wounded lying about, many of them I knew, and first one then another would ask me to give him water or do some other favor for him. While thus occupied, Dr. P. told me to stay with him, that I was not able to go on the field—that I would be captured. There was no one to help him, and I turned surgeon, *pro tempore*. I was not able to do much, but rendered all the assistance in my power. Part of my business was to put patients under the influence of chloroform. I kept my handkerchief saturated all the time, and was often dizzy from the effects of it myself. It was about one o'clock in the day, when I got there.[5]

---

4. Jean was a common material in homemade uniforms for the Western soldiers and, as throughout the Confederacy, attempts to color the cloth gray with ersatz dyes most often resulted in a butternut color. Jackman's reference to "Brown Jeans" probably also betrays a middle-class Kentuckian's slight disdain for the unsophisticated and ill-educated boys from Alabama, Mississippi, and Tennessee.

5. The diary of Captain John W. Caldwell, commanding Company A of the 5th (9th) Kentucky, and later to be the regiment's colonel and, after the war, Jackman's law instructor, reveals even more of the scene at the regimental hospital. His arm had just been broken by a bullet:

All day long the battle raged. Occasionally there would be a lull
for a short time; but the cannon were never entirely hushed. They
would break out in increased thunder, and the roar of musketry
would roll up and down the lines, vibrating almost regularly from
one extreme to the other. All day long the ambulances continued to
discharge their loads of wounded. At last night set in, and the musketry ceased; but the Federal gunboats continued shelling awhile after dark. Nearly midnight when we got through with the wounded.
A heavy rain set in. I was tired, sick, and all covered with blood. But
I was in far better fix than many that were there. I sat on a medicine
chest in the surgeon's tent, and "nodded" the long night through.

April 7th. With the dawn came the roar of battle; but the combat
did not wax very warm until later in the day. Early, all the wounded
that could walk, were given passes to go to the rear, and those not
able to walk, were placed in wagons, and started for Corinth. Many
poor fellows were not able to be moved at all. Once that morning, a
body of Federal cavalry came close enough to fire on us, tearing up
the tents, but fortunately hurting no one. Dr. P. and I were standing
close together talking, when a ball passed between our noses, which
instantly stopped our conversation. We soon hung up strips of red
flannel to prevent further accidents of the kind. A little after the
middle of the day, the battle raged terribly—it was the last struggle
of the Confederates, ending in defeat. Soon after, I saw Gen'l
Beauregard,[6] accompanied by one or two of his staff, ride leisurely
back to the rear, as cool and unperturbed as if nothing had happened. A line was being formed in the rear of us, and we had to
move. Jim B.[7] and I put the only remaining wounded of our regiment who could be moved, into a large spring wagon, and started

---

After wandering about a good deal over battlefield I succeeded in finding our Hospital. Though I was fresh from the field on which my men had fallen, I was totally
unprepared for the sight which presented itself there. All of the wounded from my
company had been carried in and many from the Regt. Merciful Heaven, what a
sight. Nearly thirty of the brave boys who had gone with me into the engagement
were lying around on the ground, torn and mangled by shot, shell and every con-
ceivable missel of death.
John W. Caldwell diary, April 6, 1862, in possession of I. Beverly Lake, Wake Forest,
N.C.
6. When General Johnston died of a mortal wound early in the afternoon of April 6,
General P. G. T. Beauregard assumed command of the army and conducted the battle
to its close.
7. James Bemiss, Company B, 9th Kentucky. Thompson, p. 817. Jackman himself
was at first believed wounded as shown by a regimental return made later in April, but

back. We had to leave some that it would have been death to put them in wagons. We hated to do so, but we could not do otherwise. The wagon was heavy, the horses were balky, and the roads were rough and muddy—besides the driver was inexperienced—all combined, we came near not getting out. B. was strong, and would tug at the wheels—I would plan, abuse the driver, and try to cheer up the horses. At last we came up with brother Jo. who was slightly wounded, and he assisted us. I believe if it had not been for him, we never would have gotten out. Night overtook us before we got far, and we drove off to the side of the road to wait till morning. The rain commenced pouring down, and continued all night. The road was in a perfect slush, and the shattered colums were plouting [plodding] over it all night. As luck would have it, a tent fly was in the wagon, and we cut bows and stretched it over the wagon-bed. I crept in, and with my feet propt up across Adjt Bell,[8] managed to sleep a little.

April 8th. Still raining awhile in the morning. On starting, we came to a little branch across the road, in which were sticking, fast in the mud, several pieces of artillery. We knew we could not cross, and had to cut out a new road through the bushes. All the army and wagons had now passed by us, save our brigade, which was covering the retreat. We got a mile or two, but at last got stuck in the mud, and immovable. I went off to a camp near by, to see if I could not get assistance. The camp was deserted. Went on a little further, hoping to find some loose horse or mule, but wearied, and came back. While gone, our Q. M.[9] had come up and put new horses in the wagon. They were in camp eating breakfast, hardtack and bacon being plentiful. On setting out, I mounted one of the old horses, barebacked, and with an old rope for a bridle. I looked Quixotic then indeed, and felt worse than the original, after his fight with the wind-mills. We got within six miles of Corinth that night. Our Q.M., who was a doctor by profession, dressed all the wounds. I slept in a corn-crib that night. Bro. Jo. had gone on to Corinth. The day ended clear and warm.

---

he later appeared on a "list of men belonging to the 5th Ky. Regiment who returned from the battle of Shiloh, Tenn. without arms," with the notation that he had been detailed to carry off the wounded from the battlefield. Jackman, Service Record.

8. First Lieutenant William Bell, mortally wounded at Shiloh. Thompson, p. 806.

9. Probably referring to Captain Henry W. Gray, assistant quartermaster of the regiment, though Thompson, p. 806, indicates that Gray had left the service prior to Shiloh.

April 9th. Cool and cloudy. Started with a new teamster. In trying to cross a stream, the wagon got stuck, but was finally engineered out. Soon after, another soldier and myself stopped at a house, and got some milk and bread for the wounded; but the wagon left us so far behind, we did not overtake it. I walked to town—the camp was just beyond. I was about "played out" when we got into camp—found nearly all of our wounded in the tents. Of those brought in the wagon, all died of their wounds but two.

April 10th. T. H.[10] came to see me. This is a temporary camp—merely where the wagon train is stopping. Muddy and disagreeable. Walked into town with T. H. and got a can of oysters. Feel better.

April 11th. Brigade came in to-day. It covered the retreat of the army, and did it, as Breckinridge promised Beauregard—"to the letter." Raining all day. The wounded, yet in camp, were sent off to the hospital. Two died afterward.

April 12th. Wrote up my Diary, which was behind. Raining all day and night. Am sick.

April 13th. Moved camp two miles from town, to a nice shady wood. Pleasant place to camp. *14th.* Went fishing, but had no luck. *15th.* Went to town and bought fishing tackle. Am weak—do no duty. *16th.* Took too much exercise yesterday. In my tent all day sick. *17th.* Feel better. Bathing before breakfast. All day fishing with Capt. G. Had little luck. *18th.* Sick again to-day. Walked too far yesterday. *19th.* No better. Rained all day—cool—disagreeable.

April 20th. Raining. Evening sent in ambulance to depot, with other sick, to be sent to Castilian Springs, Miss.[11] We had hay put down on the floor of a box-car to lie down on. Rested better than usual that night.

April 21st. Sick train did not leave Corinth until 6 P.M. to-day. Arrived at Grand Junction, 50 miles, at midnight and lay over. Took breakfast at a hotel with Lt. S. and Billie B.[12] Met with T. H., who is also going to the Springs. At 10 o'clock left on the Miss. Central. At Holly Springs, which is a nice place, we stopped for dinner. I dined

---

10. Very possibly Thomas H. Ellis, third sergeant of Company B. Thompson, p. 816.

11. Central Mississippi had numerous natural springs used as resorts and recuperation spots, Castilian Springs, near Durant, among them. On a muster roll dated April 30, 1862, Jackman appears "absent—sick at Castilian Spring since April 21." Jackman, Service Record.

12. Second Lieutenant G. C. Schaub, Company B, and William Bishop, Company C, 9th Kentucky. Thompson, pp. 815, 826.

off butter-milk alone—I wanted nothing else. After night got to Durant, our stopping place. By some mistake, our car was taken on to Goodman or Canton, being asleep, I don't know which, but was brought back by the up passenger. At 11 to-night we are at Durant, still in the car. We passed through many nice little towns to-day. The country on the railroad is productive, and under high state of cultivation. Saw many pretty ladies.

April 23d. Early went out in town, a small village, and looking cadaverous, a lady called me in and gave me a nice breakfast of milk & bread &c. While out on this expedition, many ladies had assembled at the cars, with provisions for the sick and wounded. The Springs are three miles from town, and the soldiers were brought out in carriages. About the middle of the forenoon, T. H., Dr. P. and myself, came out in a carriage. The boys had a bottle of "Hoosletter,"[13] and were quite merry. I am in a room on the 2d floor, occupied by "Morgan's men," the boys I came with, belonging to that "lay-out." Morgan's men are quite a curiosity to the people down here.[14]

The building is a two-story frame with "wings," "ells" etc., and is accommodating nearly three hundred sick and wounded-nearly all Kentuckians. The grounds are tastefully arranged about the springs, and the scenery, in the vicinity, is romantic. There was lately a female school kept in this place—was broken up, to convert the building into a hospital. The principal is our steward. The water of the springs is chalybeate. This evening had some pleasant conversation with ladies.

April 24th. When I got up in the morning, I walked out on the upper gallery, and could look down on the preparations for breakfast, the tables being set out in the yard. I did not like the appearance of the bacon and corn-bread—my appetite did not crave such delicacies (?)—so I proposed to T. H. and D. P. to walk out a short distance in the country and get breakfast. I craved milk. My constitution was wasted, and about all I needed was proper diet. In about a half a mile we came to quite an humble looking residence; but on stopping

---

13. "Hoosletter," its derivation obscure, was only one of a host of nicknames for whiskey used by the soldiers.

14. John Hunt Morgan's squadron of 160 cavalrymen had fought on the left of the brigade at Shiloh and done well, but their burgeoning fame probably came more from their depredations and antics behind the lines, for which Breckinridge had already had to discipline them. Davis, p. 53.

at the gate, we were invited in and were treated with great hospitality. The lady's husband was in the army, and she thought it very strange we did not know him. The old pipe-smoking grandmother was in the "corner," and she held up her hands in wonder, when informed that we had never met her sons John and "Jeems" who were in the Virginia army. The rosy cheeked daughter, in the mean time, had prepared us breakfast. I did justice to the butter-milk. No pay would be accepted; but we made arrangements to have milk sent us daily to the hospital, for which we were to remunerate them.

April 25th. Raining all day—cool in the evening. Very quiet here, and having been in turmoil so long, am pleased with the place.

April 26th. Day of sunshine. Many ladies have visited the hospital to-day. With woman's kindness, they ministered many comforts to the sick and wounded. The change of diet, with rest, is giving me strength daily. *27th.* Sunday, and many visitors. Had divine service, the chaplain of my reg't officiating.

April 28th. With four others, have come to Mr. Gray's on a fishing excursion. This evening had good luck fishing, and had an abundance of fish for supper. Staying with Mr. G. to-night, who is a fine old planter, and his wife, the cleverest of ladies.

April 29th. Fished until evening, then returned to the hospital with a fine lot of fish, which caused us to receive a warm welcome from the other "rats." My health improving.

May 1st. Visited Mr. Gray's to fish. Had a fine lot for supper. *May 2d.* Went fishing to Jack Lake, but had no luck. Evening, returned to hospital.

May 5th. Walked to Durant. Saw Lt. S.[15] Shall start for the front to-morrow. *May 6th.* Last night had severe pain in right side and cramp. To-day in bed. The old Dr. says I ate too much. *7th.* Feel better to-day. The old Dr. who accused me of eating too much— which is not so—is very sick to-day *from eating an overdose of eggs.* My time to laugh. *9th.* Light fever in evening. *10th.* Am not well. Time drags heavily—nothing to read. *13th.* Improving.

May 14th. Brown[16] died in our room this morning. How little feeling soldiers have sometimes! Though ever willing to help a comrade while living, when dead, there is never much shedding of tears for them. We were all standing around Brown's bed, and when he drew

---

15. Schaub.
16. Possibly Thomas Brown. Company C, 4th Kentucky. Thompson, p. 639.

his last breath, one of the boys bent over him, observed him for a moment, and said: "He never will draw another breath *as long as he lives.*" This was said so simply, the whole room roared out in laughter. We buried B. in the evening. Many are dying here. Intend to go to the front in a few days. 16th. Shall start for Corinth to-morrow.

May 17th. Came to Durant on horseback this morning. At. Mr. C's all day with Lt. S. When I left, in the evening, Mrs. C. put me up something nice to eat while on the road. Took the train for Grand Junction at 10 P.M.

May 18th. On the road all night. Took breakfast at Holly Springs. Got to G. J. at 10 a.m. and changed cars for Corinth, where the train arrived at 1 P.M. Being sunday, all quiet. Soon found the regiment, which had moved camp. Found the boys all well. The camp is about two miles west of town, and about the same distance from the fortifications on the left wing. The boys have been working on the fortifications. Soon after I had left the brigade marched out on the right expecting a battle. They represent having seen a hard time, the weather being wet & cold.

May 20th. Heavy cannonading all day, in front. Our brigade being held in reserve, we having nothing to do with the fighting going on daily. We'll not "go in" until there is a general row. *21st.* On drill for the first time in several months. Ordered to cook two days rations. Prospect of a fight.

May 22d. Beautiful sunny day. Early, the long roll was beat, and we fell in, with two days rations in haversacks. All equipped for battle. When we moved off, a long train of ambulances followed us, each having the red flag out, which indicated a battle—a long ordnance train also followed us. The infirmary corps marched in the rear of each regiment, bearing their white litters, which, perhaps, would soon be stained with human gore. Once, while fronted on the road, Gen'l Breckinridge rode by. He was dressed in citizen suit, with a broad rimmed felt hat on.[17] He passed our reg't first, and the boys cheered him. He said: "Boys, I shall try and be with you more to-day, than before." When asked, after the battle of Shiloh, why he was not with his old brigade more during the battle, he said that he

---

17. Dress was informal among most of the Western generals. Breckinridge, when in action, preferred a uniform coat of dark blue "Kentucky jeans," or else what he called his "battle shirt," a blue check made for him by his wife. William C. Davis, *Breckinridge: Statesman, Soldier, Symbol* (Baton Rouge, La: Louisiana State University Press, 1974), pp. 305, 383 (hereinafter cited as Davis, *Breckinridge*).

knew the Kentucky boys would fight without the presence of their
Maj. Gen'l—and that he was needed more on other parts of the
field. This was considered quite a compliment.[18] When passing the
other regiments, all cheered him loudly. Two or three miles beyond
the fortifications, on the left wing, we formed line of battle. We
marched some distance then, which was very difficult, on account
of the under-growth. We were the third line. When close to the enemy, halted, lounged about, waiting for Van Dorn[19] and Price[20] to
open on the right; but they failed to accomplish the flank movement intended, and we marched back to camp that evening, without
any battle.

May 23d. Raining all day. Reading one of Scott's novels. *24th.*
Heavy firing on the right. *25th.* At the interment of S. S.[21] who died
of wound recd. at Shiloh. A "father" was present to read the burial
service. He was buried with military honors.

May 26th and 27th. Cooking four days rations. Mystery about the
movements. Nearly all the tents taken from us—12 to a tent. Some
say retreat—some say fight. Old "Beaure"[22] knows what he is about.

May 28th. In the morning broke up camp and started the wagon
train to the rear, then marched out to the trenches, where we lay in
reserve all day. Our brigade is the reserve of the division, and our
reg't the reserve of the brigade. Heavy skirmishing along the whole
line to-day. In the evening, the enemy were close enough to throw
two solid shot over us. To-night all quiet. Cannot tell whether we are
going to wait for an attack, or retreat. Have been suffering for water
all day.

May 29th. Have not moved to-day. Little skirmishing in front—
very quiet. Have been suffering for water all day. The wagon train
has now been gone two days. A little after dark, all of our troops fell
back, but we did not know it, at the time.

---

18. At Shiloh, General Johnston had early ordered the Kentucky Brigade detached
from the rest of Breckinridge's small corps, and the two were not reunited until the
end of the fighting on April 6. Breckinridge was promoted from brigadier to major
general on April 14, 1862. Davis, *Breckinridge,* p. 315.

19. Major General Earl Van Dorn.

20. Major General Sterling Price.

21. Sylvester Smith, Company B, 9th Kentucky, died on May 23, 1862. Thompson,
p. 823.

22. Jackman's spelling of Beauregard's nickname is rather high toned in an army
whose soldiers spelled very phonetically, if they spelled at all. The general was usually
referred to as "Old Borey."

May 30th. Last night at 12 o'clock, the order came around in whispers to fall in—to be silent about it. It was so dark we could not see our file-leaders. After much trouble, the regiment was formed. All day we had been speculating whether we were to go out of the fortifications and hazard a battle, wait an attack, or retreat. Falling in at that hour, we knew that we were going out to fight, or retreat one [or the other] and that we would soon know. We were in suspense—all were silent and anxious. Just as the column started to move, someone set an old tent on fire, which suddenly blazed up, dispersing the darkness for a moment, and revealed the head of the column moving towards the trenches. The light dazzled only a moment on the aslanted guns of the gray column, as it wended through the column of old oaks, then died away leaving inky darkness. When we got up to the trenches—had been lying in the rear—we found all the troops had left them. We moved on parallel with the works towards the sally-port. Suspense! Would we go out, or turn off on the road to the left? We moved on the road to the left, and a hum of subdued voices came from the retreating column. There was no longer suspense. If we had gone out at the sally-port, all would have been as cheerful marching towards the enemy, as they now were, retreating from him. The "orphans" are always cheerful, whether sharing the glories of victory, or in the midst of disaster.[23] We soon came up with a section of Cobb's[24] battery, which was to stay with our regiment, now the rear guard. Our road led from the left wing, and a little to the left of town. The night was so dark, the artillery and our two ambulances kept getting against trees and stumps, delaying us. We had to cross bridges over swamps and some of the boys fell off into the mud. I could always travel well of nights, and while others were tumbling over stumps and roots, I kept my footing.

When we got on the Kossuth road, in sight of Corinth, to the rear, gray morning had come, and we halted to rest. Soon the sun "came peeping over the hills," and no troops were to be seen, save a few

---

23. This is Jackman's first use, and the earliest known postwar usage of the sobriquet "orphans" in referring to the First Kentucky Brigade. As used here, it is almost certainly a later addition made during one of his transcriptions of his diary notes, probably that done in April 1865 at Washington, Georgia. Since Jackman's diary was substantially complete by the summer of 1865, this may be taken as the first—and to date only—evidence that at least some of the Kentuckians were already using the term "orphan brigade" during the war.

24. Captain Robert L. Cobb's battery was raised in Kentucky and attached to the brigade from its first organization, remaining with it to the end of the war.

cavalry scouts. Ever since the signal gun had broken the stillness of the night, our troops had been marching away. After daylight the commissary stores, that had been left behind, were fired, and high up rose the black pillow of smoke. All was quiet as death. A few wounded and broken down cavalry horses were quietly cropping grass on the common, and about the only animated nature to be seen. We fell in, and marched to the Tuscumbia, 5 miles from town, and filed off the road and stacked arms in line of battle. The two howitzers were planted on the road. We took some breakfast. In the afternoon, moved across the river, and our cavalry scouts having come over, the bridge was burned and trees cut across the road. Here we joined the 22d Miss. of the same division. To-night all quiet. Bivouacking in line of battle. Rations short.

May 31st. All quiet this morning. A scout from the enemy came to the opposite side of the river, but went back. The Tuscumbia is a small stream, but deep. The swamps on either side impassable. At 4 P.M. fell in to march, but the order was countermanded. Late a heavy skirmish at the bridge above us.

June 1st. Early in the afternoon, heavy shower of rain. Was detailed on a scout to go down the river, and had a muddy tramp—saw nothing. At 4 P.M., fell in and took up our line of march on the Kossuth road. Our regiment, the 22d Miss. and the section of Cobb's battery, with a few cavalry, composed the rear guard on the road. The command was kept well closed up, and was under the comd. of Col. H. As the sun was setting, passed through the little town of Kossuth. The night set in dark, and we pushed forward, never stopping. Just before midnight, I was so tired, not having marched any for a long time, and not feeling well, I had to "tumble out" into a fence corner to rest—one of the boys "fell by the way" with me—and the column moved on. We were both soon napping. We had fallen out just as the column was turning off the main road, on another to the right. In a short time I was waked by a party of cavalry riding by, taking the straight road, and from the rattling of their sabres, I took them to be Federals. As soon as they were gone, I roused my companion, and being rested, pushed on. There were several roads branching off; but fortunately, the artillery was in the rear of the troops and we could, by stooping low, see the broad tracks of the wheels in the dust. This guided us on the proper road. We heard the report of a gun, and when we cought up, found a cavalryman had accidentally shot himself through the leg. The scouts reported the

enemy half a mile off, on the other road. When we cought up, the
reg't had just halted to rest, and I lay down, (12 oclock). I slept an
hour of the best sleep in my life. We were roused at 1 o'clock, and
pushed on from that until daylight, when we stopped a short time to
rest. I was tired enough.

June 2d. Marched until noon, when we halted to rest an hour.
Here all the roads came together, and we were joined by several
other regiments. The Federal cavalry was reported to be in front of
us, on the flanks—and of course following us. We drew some hardtack and bacon, and ate dinner. When our hour was out, ordered to
fall in. We saw the field officers riding about looking "blue"; but we
were too near worn out to pay any attention to impending danger.
The enemy was reported closing in around us, and Col. H., who was
still in comd. of the rear, commenced forming his lines. Lt. Col.
Johnson—assigned while the 2d was in prison—was in command of
our regiment.[25] The boys called him "Uncle Bob." Uncle Bob is a
clever brave man, but utterly ignorant of military tactics. Uncle Bob
ordered us to fall in. Now he was not at all afraid, but a little excited.
Not moving off immediately, some of the boys, being worn out, sat
down in ranks. Uncle Bob seeing it, ripped out an oath, and said the
regiment didn't know the "first principles of drilling." All the boys
being brought to their feet, Uncle Bob gave the order, "right face"—
not a man moved. He grew purple with rage, thinking he had a little
mutiny on hand. "Why don't you move?" shouted Uncle Bob. Someone remarked to him that we could not, until we "came to a
shoulder."[26] He "simmered," and said something about all being lia-
ble to make mistakes. The boys were full of laugh, and knew that he
would make other mistakes, and resolved to show them to him. After
marching us around through the woods awhile, he at last came to
where he wished us to rest in line of battle, and gave the order to
"front." We did so, but our *faces were set from the enemy instead* of
towards them. Uncle Bob again drew himself up, and wanted to know
what in the h—l we were doing. "Didn't you order us to front?"
asked one of the captains, respectfully saluting. "Yes; but I wanted
you to face this way," cried Uncle Bob. The regiment could hold in
no longer, and roared out in laughter. Col. H. about that time came

---

25. Lieutenant Colonel Robert A. Johnson, 2d Kentucky Infantry, had been
detached from his regiment before it went to Fort Donelson, where it surrendered.
Thompson, p. 548.

26. Jackman means "shouldered arms," the marching position for the rifle.

up, and took command. The regiment moved out on the road and continued the march. Uncle bob slunk back to the rear of the reg't, looking like he had been doing worse things than teaching us the "first principles of drilling." Before that, it seems the colonels, in a council of war, had gotten into disputes about something and Col. H. declared he would take his regiment and go on through, enemy or no enemy. The commander of the 22d Miss. said he would follow him with his regiment—I believe all the rest followed. When we got to Black Land, three miles, we found the federal cavalry had just left. The day was hot and we could get no water fit to drink. Late in the evening, had a heavy rain storm, which rendered the roads so slippery we could hardly march. Just before sundown, we came to our lines, and Gen'l Breckinridge was surprised to see us—had given us up as lost, knowing the Federal cavalry was swarming about our way. At sunset, came to our wagon train near Baldwyn, camped in a low swampy place. We were a tired set of boys. I was in a good condition to sleep in mud and water.

June 3d. Moved camp a short distance into an old field—not a shade-tree standing in it. Water very scarce, and indifferent.

June 5th. All the tents taken from us, but three to the company. Cooked four days rations for a march. There is no rest for the soldier.

•3•

Get Out of the Wilderness: Vicksburg, Louisiana, and North to Kentucky

The summer of 1862 was a dreadful one for the Kentuckians. They spent only a few days in Tupelo before being ordered to Vicksburg to aid in the defense of the city against a Union advance. They arrived there only to endure weeks of almost constant shelling from Yankee gunboats. Some of the men briefly turned sailor when the Rebel ram CSS Arkansas needed crewmen to help her resist the enemy vessels. As many as sixty of the Kentuckians helped operate the ram and man her guns that July.

The activity helped take their minds off the terrible sickness that prevailed in the camps during the hot, humid summer. The only good news for them was the return of Colonel Helm from sick leave. Helm assumed command of the brigade containing the 4th and 5th (9th) regiments. In late July Breckinridge was ordered to take his command south to Baton Rouge, Louisiana, and both brigades of Bluegrass regiments went with him. On August 5 they fought a tough battle and were victorious on the field, but when Federal gunboats shelled them, they were forced to withdraw. The brigades then moved to Port Hudson, where the men began construction of massive fortifications. These would become the southern anchor of a length of Rebel-dominated river that stretched northward to Vicksburg.

Fate often toyed cruelly with the Kentuckians, and in September it did so again when they were ordered to join with Braxton Bragg's Army of Tennessee in an invasion of their homeland.

Cheering and singing that they were going back to Kentucky, the brigades moved off on an arduous trek to Knoxville, Tennessee. They arrived there too late to join Bragg, who had already gone into the Bluegrass and was even then being forced back out of the state. Breckinridge and his command came within sight of Cumberland Gap, with the mountains of eastern Kentucky seen dimly in the distance, when orders came on October 19 to turn around and go back. It was as close to their homeland as they would ever come during the war.

Worse was the fact that the twelve-month enlistments of some regiments expired in September. On the 22d of that month, while en route for Knoxville, some companies of the 5th (9th) mutinied and refused to obey orders, protesting the rumor that they would be forcibly kept in service after their enlistments were over. Breckinridge and Hunt quelled the uprising, only to have it recur in the 6th Kentucky on October 8. Only a mixture of eloquence, patience, and willpower enabled Breckinridge to put it down, and eventually the mutineers all reenlisted for three years.

Despite their disappointment at not reaching Kentucky, there was a little good news for the Kentuckians in Tennessee. Colonel Roger Hanson of the 2d Kentucky rejoined them with his regiment, taking brigade command from Helm, who had been wounded at Baton Rouge. And on October 26, 1862, the regiments were reunited when Breckinridge put the 2d, the 4th, the 6th, and the newly redesignated 9th Infantries together again, along with two Kentucky batteries and, for a time, the 41st Alabama. It was fortunate they were all together, for while they encamped at Murfreesboro that December, a storm such as none of them had yet experienced was on the way.

At Tupelo

June 6th.—Reveille at 3 o'clock. Loaded our remaining equippage, and the train started towards Tupelo. The regiment moved into the woods, and bivouacked for the day and night.

June 7th.—Fell in at sunrise, and marched towards Tupelo. As the division meandered through the long lanes, the sun reflecting on thousands of polished guns, I was struck with the scene. There seemed a tide of melted silver flowing on by the green fields.— There *was* a good deal of *lead* along, but [it] was not melted. Soon the day got hot, and dust obscured all such scenery. I had on a new pair of shoes, which blistered my feet. Once I pulled them off; but the sand was so hot, I could not stand it. I managed to keep up all day. Suffered for water. Marched 20 miles.

June 8th.—Marched 12 miles to Tupelo, then 5 miles west, and bivouacked. Sore feet, mine. Tupelo is a small dirty looking town, on the Mobile and Ohio rail road. The war, I presume, has given it something of its dirty appearance.

June 10th.—Established camp 7 miles west of town, in an old field, grown up with persimmon bushes. Hot place. Old Sol's batteries play directly upon us—there can be no dodging.

June 11th.—Hot!!! Edibles are running low in camp—bill of fare: corn-bread pickled beef,—very bad,—and molasses. Sometimes we get something from the country people. Prices current: Spring chickens, 50 to 75 cts; tough hens, 80 cts to $1: old roosters, $1 to $1.25: turkeys: $1.50 to $2.00; old ganders, $1.50: goose, same: vegitables— 50 cts for peeping over the fence into the garden!

June 13th.—Our battalion drill at 2 P.M. Hot work. All the time, while encamped at Tupelo, had regular drills, and the weather could not have been hotter. There was only one small spring to water the brigade, which was guarded, and no one could get water, save at the regular water calls.

June 19th.—Gen'l Breckinridge's division being ordered west, marched at an early hour, with three days rations in haversacks. At 1 P.M. got to Pontotoc, 15 miles, and bivouacked near town. Though my feet were very sore, went blackberry hunting that evening.

June 20th.—Mchd. early. Cut my shoes so they did not hurt my feet quite so bad, and marched with greater ease. A very hot and dusty march of 18 miles, brought us to LaFayette Springs, late in the afternoon. Springs not much improved. I believe a ten-pin alley is all the improvements to be seen, with a little stone house over the springs, which are chalybiate. Had to cook rations to-night.

June 21st.—On the road early. Our course led mostly over pine ridges to-day. Very hot and dusty. The 4th Ky. marched in front, and tried to march us down. About the middle of the day, our boys got mad, and commenced double-quicking and cheering. Before that my feet were so sore I could scarcely walk, but in the excitement, I forgot my feet. We ran over the 4th. and went on. At 2 P.M., bivouacked near a nice stream for bathing.

June 22d.—Marched 7 miles, and camped. Went out foraging with B. Remained in camp several days, and blackberrys being plentiful, we lived well. Had a blackberry cobbler for dinner nearly every day, and G.A.[1] would make stacks of pies. Near Abbeville, Miss.

June 25th.—Had reveille before day light, and by sun-rise, our column was on the road. Five miles brought us to Abbeville, on the Miss. Central. The little village looks woe-begone now. When I passed it last spring it was a nice looking little town. Armies, whether friend or foe, desolate a country. The distance from here to Tupelo is 60 miles. We have just gone through a hot and dusty tramp. Bivouacked near town, and waiting for transportation on the rail road.

June 28th.—Late in the evening, our regiment marched to the depot to take the cars. A flat car next the engine fell to our company. We also had to pile our camp equipage on the same car, and when all things were ready for the whistle to blow, it was piled up mountain-high, indiscriminately, with men, tents, camp-chests, camp-kettles, etc. At 8 P.M., whirled away towards Jackson. We had the benefit of all the cinders and sparks from the locomotive, and many had their clothing burnt. At midnight, lay over at Grenada for daylight.

June 29th.—Got to Canton at noon, and lay over an hour or two. I went to a hotel for dinner. Bought a ticket, after much crowding, and went into the dining hall with a jam. Was fortunate enough to get a plate, and commenced bawling at a waiter to bring something to eat. Now there were few waiters, and many fierce soldiers yelling at them, making the eyes of the said waiters grow large and white, from fear, and I did not get my roast beef for sometime. At last it came, and though I always considered my teeth good, yet I could not even make a print on the piece brought me. Could get nothing else to eat on my plate, and seeing all the rest turn waiters for themselves, I took my plate, and also went to the cook-room. There I found a crowd of soldiers, with plates in their hands, standing around the cook, who was preparing the last thing in the house fit to eat—a beef heart. *My heart failed me,* and I went back to the train, and dined out of my haversack. Train arrived at Jackson the middle afternoon,

---

1. George Ambrose, Company B, 9th Kentucky Infantry. Thompson, p. 816.

and we moved out on Vicksburg road about sundown. Ran as far as Clinton, 12 miles, and the train switched off till morning. During the whole trip the sun was very hot, and we had no protection from the heat, being on a flat car.

June 30th.—Train moved out for Vicksburg in the morning, and until the middle of the afternoon running to V.—Very hot day. The trees all along the road, hung with long gray moss. The train first ran down near town, but backed to 4 mile Bridge, where we dismounted the iron-horse and went into camp. We pitched our tents in beautiful dell, under wide-spreading liveoaks. After our hot trip it was quite a luxury to extend out on the grass in the cool shade. We lacked water, though a brook had run through the valley; but now only stagnant pools remained. We had to drink this water, which had a sweet-brackish taste. Across the valley, or ravine, was a high trestlework which the iron-horse was continually crossing. Our camp was nearly under this bridge, and I was often waked up at night, by them puffing and shrieking overhead, while crossing the bridge. My friend J. H.[2] the *fastidious* gentleman at home, this evening on detail to dig a well, near the Col's tent, on the margin of the brook. *He looks well.* Has off his shoes, and his briches are rolled up nearly to the knees— said briches have suffered greatly in the rear—and now that he is in the shade, his hat is thrown off, and his soiled shirt is open wide at the collar. He is not *very* fastidious now, but is merry withal—is singing and toiling away with pick and spade, in quest of water, which I hope he will find—that is, he and his fellow-workers.

July 1st. During the forenoon occasionally the boom of cannon would come over the hills from the direction of the river. At 4 P.M. marched into the city, 4 miles, and halted at the court house, which is in the center of town. Here I first saw the "father of waters," and three miles below the city, saw the Federal fleet. Their mortar boats were perhaps closer, having covered the rigging with limbs of trees, and crept up along the far bank; but now the leaves had died, and they could be plainly seen. I also saw the smoke away up the river, where the "Lincum gun-boats lay."[3] About sundown detailed for picket duty, and was posted upon the river bank above town. Was

---

2. James Hunter, Company B, 9th Kentucky Infantry, was later killed at Chickamauga. Thompson, p. 820.

3. Jackman is quoting from Henry Clay Work's 1862 song, "Kingdom Coming," meaning that this is almost certainly a passage written from memory, probably in 1865, since the Work tune was as yet hardly known in the South.

after dark, and very dark, before we got to our position, and had great difficulty in marching, the bluffs were so steep and rugged. Though the day had been very hot, yet the wind swept down the river at night, cold and disagreeable. Relieved at daylight, or rather we were drawn off, and we returned to the regiment, which had bivouacked above town (half a mile) during the night.

July 2d. In the forenoon all quiet. As evening came on, moved down near the city in a ravine close to where "whistling Dick" was mounted.[4] The upper fleet soon after commenced shelling from mortar-boats, and it seems they knew where we were, for most of the shells fell about our ravine. There can be no dodging from mortar shells. One has to stand bolt upright, like a duck in the rain. Dr. P. and others got into a sink-hole for shelter, but came near being buried alive by a shell. First we would hear the mortars go boom, boom, boom, away over the bend of the river, and soon after could hear the shells whining high up in air, as they came circling over, and then they would come shrieking down. If they burst in air, first little tufts of smoke could be seen, then the loud reports as they were burst into fragments, and immediately the jagged pieces would commence humming down, different sized pieces making the different notes in the demoralizing music. I felt sorry for the inhabitants. Those that were left in the city commenced leaving town. I noticed one lady going out a street with five or six little children about her that were gambling along unconscious, it seemed, of danger, until a bomb burst almost in their midst, when they all huddled about their mother for protection. Late in the evening marched to the lower end of the city, and after dark went down and bivouacked about the lower water battery. Nearly all night long the lower mortar fleet was throwing shells over us into the city. Could first see the flash, then came the report of the mortar, and almost with the thunder, came the sound of the rushing shell until it reached the top of the circle, then could hear it no longer (but could see the light of the fuse as it were a meteor traversing the heavens) and presently could hear it crashing among the houses up-town.

---

4. "Whistling Dick" has been the subject of much controversy, but was apparently an eighteen-pound, iron siege gun that had been rifled and reinforced at the breech and so named because of the peculiar sound its shells made in flight. Warren Ripley, *Artillery and Ammunition of the Civil War* (New York: Van Nostrand, Reinhold, 1970), pp. 30–31.

July 3d.—Before daylight moved back into the railroad cut. Both fleets shelling all day, but this time did not exactly get our range. Expecting to catch "fits" to-morrow.

July 4th.—To-day we all expected a severe bombardment, but there was not a shell thrown into the City. The fleets fired 33 guns as a salute.

July 5th.—Returned to camp in the evening, marching out on the railroad. There was no shelling until after we left

July 7th.—Marched into town again. Troops have to be kept here all the time to support the batteries. We relieved Preston's[5] brigade. Remained until the 11th. Shells falling on the city all the time; but, fortunately, never in range. We had a good time, having nothing to do but lie around in the shade, eat figs, water-melons, etc. I prefer staying in the city, to camp. Here we get good cistern water to drink and are now used to the shells.

July 13th.—The regiment marched into the city. Am left in camp on detail.

July 14th.—Struck tents, loaded the wagons, and moved camp to the suburbs of town. Established in a grassy ravine a few trees standing about to lend us shade. The day has been very hot. We shall have cistern water hauled to us all the time, now. Regiment came in at dark.

July 15th.—At 9 A.M. heard firing up the river, and went up on the bluff to see the cause. Could see a commotion on the upper fleet which was sending up a dark cloud of smoke, and firing. Presently we saw the C.S. Arkansas coming around the bend, and soon after landed at the levee under our batteries, where there was an enthusiastic crowd assembled to welcome her. Late in the evening marched to our old position—about the rail road cut, below the depot, or rather, the engine house. The air was full of shells. Just as we were filing off the railroad, up a street, where there was a high bluff that could protect us, in a measure from the shells, all the upper batteries opened and were replied to by the upper fleet dropping down before the city. The first intimation we had of this movement, one of those long conical shells 2 feet in length, and 10 inches in diameter came shrieking just over our heads, making something [like] the noise of a man screaming in agony. Soon the fight became

---

5. Brigadier General William Preston. His brigade mentioned here, of course, is the one composed of the 3d, 6th, and 7th Kentucky, Cobb's battery, and an Alabama unit, after the Kentucky brigade was split in half in May. Davis, p. 104.

general The morter fleet above and below filled the air with bursting shells; the fleet vomited forth iron and flame: our batteries thundered, making the very earth tremble, hot shot from the fleet were flying through the air, mimicking the fork-tongued lightening, and the flash of artillery, made the night as light as day. To heighten the grand scene, some buildings up-town took fire from hot missiles and a pillar of flame pierced the very heavens. As the storm-cloud passes, so did this. Soon a perfect silence brooded over the city, and we went to sleep. I hardly think the firing lasted an hour.

July 18th.—About 12 M., a piece of shell wounded one of the Col's badly, while lying in his tent. Many of our tents have been cut up, but no-one hurt, until to-day. One night, a party was in the Q.M.'s tent playing "poker" and while piling up the "chips", a piece of shell came through the tent scattering the "tea-party", as well as the "chips". No body hurt. In the evening, regiment in town on duty. The morter fleets keep up shelling. They have regular hours: Commence at 10 A.M. and continue until 12, when they knock off for dinner; then commence at 2 P.M., and continue shelling until night. One day "Mc."[6] said, when they had stopped for dinner, that he hopes they would have "bony fish" to eat so they would be a long time getting through.

July 21st.—Reg't in town on duty. At night, our Company deployed on the riverbank, with Co. G., to picket. While in camp, the mosquitoes never bothered us on account of the camp-fires, but when we would get out on duty like this, where we were not even allowed to smoke a pipe, the mosquitoes would give us "fits." I had often heard of their being so large in Texas that they carried a brick-bat under their wings with which to whet their bills, but I never believed the story, until I came to Vicksburg.

July 22d.—Companies withdrawn before daylight; but a few of us were left until after sun-up to watch the river to see that no one crossed. We were stationed about 60 yards apart, and ordered to secrete ourselves, but watch vigilantly. I hid away "neath a rosy bower," by a little white cottage, now tenantless, and waited for morn. Soon the gray light of morning came—then came the "powerful King of

---

6. In a postwar article by Jackman, "Vicksburg in 1862," *Southern Bivouac*, III (September 1884), p. 7, it is clear that "Mc" in this episode is really Ed Clayland, Company K, 2d Kentucky. He had escaped capture at Donelson and attached himself to the 9th Kentucky, with which he stayed through the summer of 1862. Thompson, p. 616.

day, rejoicing in the east". The landscape was beautiful, and I was admiring it, peeping out from my "rosy bower"—and occasionally looking out of the corner of my eye at two large frigates, just below me, their sides bristling with guns, and wondering what would be the consequence, were they to give us a broadside—when "Whistling Dick" & Co. commenced thundering up the river and I forsook my "bower" to see what was going on. I saw "Essex" coming down and give the Arkansaw a broadside. After that she closed all her ports. About that time the Corporal came along withdrawing us and we started up-town. Before we got up the bank, a heavy water-battery commenced firing over our heads at the Essex, and the concussion was so great from the balls passing over, that we were almost lifted off the ground. The Essex* kept on her way, our guns peppering her; but, the balls would bounce off, as rain-drops from a duck's back. To-day our regiment lounged about the grounds of S.S. Prentiss' Castle.[8] The place shows him to have been a man of great taste, as well as orator. We were conspicuous here, and were shelled away in the evening, about the time we were starting for camp.

July 24th.—In town again. Not well—have been feeling badly several days. At night, a detail was made to report to the Arkansas for duty, and I had to go from our company. Twas first thought we were to make up the crew, and one fellow objected so much that he ran off. We all objected to such a fate, and Lieut. McC.[9] in charge of the whole detail from the brigade, said that if such was the case, he would resist. We had to wait until morning for all the detail to get together.

July 25th.—The Lt. found out that we were to do some work at the Arkansaw, and as I did not feel well enough to work, tried to get off, but could not. Went down to the boat and reported, and the Captain[10] told us that we would not be wanted until dark, so we went

*Reported at the time as the Essex, but afterwards it was stated that it was the Queen of the West.[7]

---

7. Jackman later changed his mind and states that it was the *Essex*, and the brigade historian agreed with him. Jackman, "Vicksburg in 1862," p. 7; Thompson, p. 116.

8. Sargent S. Prentiss, noted Mississippi statesman.

9. There was no lieunent in the brigade whose surname began with "Mc." Lieutenant Robert B. Matthews of Cobb's battery led the contingent of Kentuckians who helped work aboard the *Arkansas*, and actually worked one of her guns in battle. *O.R.*, series I, volume 15, pp. 1122–24.

10. Captain Isaac Brown commanded the *Arkansas*.

up-town and took up quarters in a large mansion then vacated. There were fifty on the detail. The boys had piano music and dancing, with plenty of books to read. About sundown, a neighboring bee-gum[11] was brought in, and we had a "sweet time." The Ram had gone up the river and did not get back until 9 P.M. We went down then, and found out our job was to coal the boat, which had to be done by carrying the coal some distance in bags. I didn't work much. Got through by midnight, and went back to our house. All day the morters had been at work, which was the last shelling done that season.

July 26th.—At daylight saw the lower fleet had gone, and the upper one just disappearing up the river. Went to camp early. That evening moved camp 2 miles from town. Am sick.

July 27th.—Attended surgeons call. Am taking intermittent fever. In the forenoon the regiment ordered to leave on the cars. Not able to go, and left in camp, which was to stand. Reg't did not get off to-day.

July 28th.—Reg't got off this morning. This evening, I learn a car in the train, on which our regiment was moving, broke down, but no one seriously hurt. I hope to follow the troops in a few days.

Remained in the camp until I left for my command Aug. 6th. I only had to take medicine two or three days, as the fever did not get a good hold upon my system. I then applied to follow the regiment, but could not get transportation. Went to Vicksburg one day, and J. O. B.[12] and I went out a short way into the country, the day before I left, after peaches—the only times I was out of camp. That camp was like all—monotonous. The evening before I left, J. O. B. and I got some reeds and made a nice bunk to sleep upon at 2 o'clock, A.M.

Aug. 6th.—All that were able, had to get up and prepare to start for the regiment. I did not regret rising from my reed bed, which was almost equal to a spring mattress, for I wanted to be off. My friend was not able to go, and could use it. After day light about 60 from the reg't able to go, went to the railroad, but we could not immediately get a train, so we came back to camp, about noon, and drew new uniforms, and other clothing, the first we had drawn for a long time. We got started in time to reach Jackson a little after dark. There were 300 or 400 men from Breckinridge's division *in transit.*

---

11. A bee-gum was—and still is—a bee hive or bee tree containing honey.

12. J. O. B. is probably John O. Bryant, Company D, 9th Kentucky. Thompson, p. 831.

Left Jackson at 8 P.M., on the G.N. & W.R.R.[13] Lay down on the floor of a box-car and went to sleep.

Aug. 7th.—Waked up just as day was dawning, and found that we were going lightening speed towards New Orleans. Dense pine forests were on either side of the road. Soon passed through Brook-Haven—a nice little town. Summit and Hazlehurst are also pretty towns. At 9 A.M., arrived at Tangipaho[14] 80 miles from New Orleans and 100 miles from Jackson, Miss. We were now in Louisiana. Camp Moore is a short distance from the station, and we disembarked and took up quarters in the Camp. Camp nicely arranged, "shanties" and tents. There is a stream circling the camp of the clearest water I ever saw. I believe it is called a river, but I don't know the name.* This is where all the Louisiana troops met to organize, before starting for the seat of war. Tangipaho is a small village, built since the railroad.

Aug. 10th.—Early started on the march for the division, encamped near Baton Rouge. There are 2 or 300 of the division along—(some that started from Vicksburg were left at Camp Moore) under the command of Lt. Col. Crump,[15] an old "Yellow-hammer",[16] I believe. Hot day. Our march led through a pine forest. Just before we stopped for the night—passed through Greensburg, the parish-town of St. Helena. Marched 10 miles to-day.

Aug. 11th. The old Colonel tried to get us to fall in and march in order; but such a dusty arrangement didn't suit us! so we divided off in squads to please ourselves. Been another hot day. Our road led through an interminable pine forest. The country is perfectly level, and there is no undergrowth to obstruct the view—can see a long way through the woods, the pines standing not very thick and straight and beautiful. The ground is covered by a carpet of green wier-grass. The country is pretty to look at; but the sand wouldn't suit an old farmer. What stillness in these pineries! You never see a

*The Tangipaho River.

---

13. The New Orleans, Galveston & Great Northern Railroad was the only connection between Jackson and New Orleans. Jackman got the "G.N." part of its abbreviation correct but must have been confused about the balance of the line's name.

14. Tangipahoa.

15. Lieutenant Colonel William N. Crump, 31st Alabama Infantry. The 31st, of course, was attached to the other "First Kentucky" brigade containing the 4th and 5th Infantries. Joseph H. Crute, Jr., *Units of the Confederate States Army* (Midlothian, Va.: Derwent Books, 1987), p. 23.

16. "Yellow-hammer" was a contemporary nickname for an Alabamian. See also Kirwan, p. 106.

bird, nor even hear a grass-hopper chirp. While marching to-day—
and a very hot one it has been—we could always see a shade ahead
of us in the road but could never reach it. The foliage of the pine
only partially breaks the sunbeams. We also suffered for water. At
night bivouacked at an old schoolhouse. Had nothing to eat but sweet
potatoes for supper.

Aug. 12th.—This morning Charlie A. of our company and Sam S.,
of the 4th., killed a "bear" in the swamp, and Billie A. and Gus M.,
having gone to a house and had bread cooked, we had a feast.[17]
There are five of the Company along—also Sam S.—and this morning we concluded to journey by ourselves—let the old Col. go on.
Marched all day through the same character of country—hot, and
water scarce. At night our little party spred their blankets under an
old oak, on the road-side, true gipsy style.

Aug. 13th.—Up early and felt greatly refreshed by "Nature's sweet
restorer." Borrowed a coffee-pot from a house, and had a hot cup of
coffee before starting. Early, passed Greenwell Springs, near which
we had stopped for the night. About noon, we got to the brigade,
camped on the Comite River, 10 miles from Baton Rouge. Soon after
we got into camp—or rather where the reg't is bivouacking—a heavy
rain set in. Having no shelter, slept in water at night.

Aug. 15th.—The commands are so reduced from sickness, to-day
companies and regiments consolidated. Our regiment joined with the
4th, and Lt. Col. Hines[18] of that regiment is in command, being
the ranking officer. Gen'l Helm[19] being wounded, Col. Trabue[20] of
the 4th Ky. is in comd, of brigade. Col. Hunt commandd. the brigade during the late battle, and was wounded.

At 5 P.M. fell in to march. At the time, a heavy rain storm was
passing over—never saw it rain harder. We marched towards Baton
Rouge. Soon the sun came out, and the evening was very warm. In
five miles of the city, we filed to the right towards Port Hudson.

---

17. Charles Applegate, Company B, Samuel Suter, Company D, William Ambrose,
Company B, and Augustus J. Moore, Company B. Thompson, pp. 817, 651, 816, 821.
A "bear" in soldier parlance usually meant a farmer's pig. Forbidden to steal livestock
from Confederate citizens, hungry soldiers often killed, cooked, and ate their prey on
the spot, euphemistically referring to it as "bear" if an officer enquired.

18. Lieutenant Colonel Andrew R. Hynes. Thompson, p. 622.

19. Brigadier General Ben Hardin Helm was accidentally wounded by his own men
in the maneuvering prior to the Battle of Baton Rouge on August 5.

20. Robert P. Trabue, colonel of the 4th Kentucky from its organization, died of
sudden illness on February 12, 1863. Thompson, pp. 406–7.

Dark set in soon after leaving the main road, and the sky became clouded. Dark is not the word to express the blackness of the night. Occasionally, a flash of lightening would reveal our file leaders, so that we could keep closed up. At bridges, too, fires were kindled by the citizens, so we could see how to cross. The dusky column would pass these lights—delving again into utter darkness. The road was uneven and in places muddy. At last we halted, and tumbled down on the wet grass, being already drenched to the skin, and slept till morning. I believe this was the darkest night I ever saw. Have been on more uncomfortable marches though.

Aug. 16th.—Very hot day. When the brigade stopped at 12, Lt. H.[21] and I were the only ones of the company up—and there were not more than 30 of both regiments together. All the balance had fallen by the wayside. Sometimes we would march through lanes a mile in length—not a shade near. Our course led through large shugar plantations, and the country looked better than usual.

Aug. 17th.—A short march brought us to within 2 miles of Port Hudson, and we camped in a swamp. Water scarce, though.

Aug. 18th.—Moved 2 miles off the road and camped in a grove of magnolia and bush trees. A "babbling brook" was near and we had an abundance of good water.

At night, when silence had come over the camp, an order came in for us to cook rations prepatory to a move for Kentucky. Soon hundreds of camp-fires blazed up and cheer upon cheer, rose from the noisy thousands. After a moment the bands all commenced playing, "Old Kentucky Home" and cheers went up with a will. After we had cooked the rations we sat around the camp-fire talking until morning. No body could sleep.

Aug. 19th. At an early hour, all the Kentucky troops, with Breckinridge at the head, took up line of march for Tangipaho, a distance of 60 or 70 miles. We moved off with a light and buoyant step, the bands playing "Get out of the Wilderness." At noon halted for dinner and on detail to help get the wagon train over a creek. A heavy rain set in and continued all evening. After marching 18 miles, we stopped for the night. Blankets and clothing wet and could get no wood, hardly, to make fires.

Aug. 20th.—On the road at 4 a.m. Marched through Clinton, in order. Quite a crowd of ladies assembled to see us. Marched 16 miles

---

21. Second Lieutenant D. W. Holtshouser, Company B, 9th Kentucky. Thompson, p. 816.

and camped on the Comite. At noon, while resting, the brigade
Q.M. came along having a lot of flour, and the boys cheered at the
sight of the barrels. We were used to musty corn meal, ground on
corn-crushers, baked without sifting, and poor blue beef.—Rained
again this evening.

Aug. 21st.—Marched to the Amite, ten miles of Tangipaho, leaving
Greensburg to the right. After in camp, the boys made a raid on a
water-melon field.

Aug. 22d.—Marched at 1 A.M., and arrived at Tangipaho, 6 a.m.
Stacked arms on the side of the rail road and waited for cars. At 9 got
on the train and moved off for Jackson, Miss., where we arrived after
dark. All the way up, the ladies were waving their hankerchiefs. We
slept at the fair-grounds.

Aug. 23d.—Marched 6 miles out on the Brandon road, where we
found our camp already established—the wagon train having arrived
from Vicksburg, a day or two before. While marching out to camp,
the weather was so hot, Col. Hines disbanded the Regt's on the road
and let every fellow take care of himself. All did not get into camp
until late in the evening.

Aug. 24th.—On fatigue all day. My health is improving some. This
regular camp does not look much like going to Kentucky soon. Our
camp is on the side of a hill, grown up with stunted oaks and tall
pines. We have plenty of good water close at hand. The weather is
very hot and sultry. Our provisions are abundant, and we can get
fruit and melons every day from citizens.

Sept. 1st.—Detailed in the Adjutant's office as clerk. Am hardly
able to do the duty of a soldier, any way.[22]

Sept. 10th.—Broke up camp and marchd to the city. At noon took
train on the Miss. Central, for Holly Springs. Got as far up as Goodman at sundown. Here the engine took water, and as the train moved
on past the tank, some fellow on the first car pulled the water-pipe
down, which caused a perfect flood of water to drench the train as it
passed slowly along. Just in front of us was a flat car on which was
Co. "H", and the water had plenty of fall. The boys rolled up in their
blankets and took it. The train stoped as the spout was over our car,
and the field-band being on top, soon a shower of drums, fifes,

---

22. Muster roll of the 9th Kentucky Infantry for September/October 1862 shows
Jackman paid on September 1 and that same day detailed as adjutant's clerk. Jackman,
Service Record.

drum-sticks, etc., came pouring down with the flood. This was great sport to all, save a captain, on the front part [of the] train, who jumped off to avoid the water, and had both his legs crushed off by the wheels.[23]

Sept. 11th.—During the morning, arrived at Holly Springs, and I tried to get my breakfast at the hotel, but failed. The train took us 16 miles above, and we got off at what we called "Cold-Water." We lived well while in this camp; a few "bears" being killed during the time. Writing all the time—Lt. O'C[24] acting adjt—made a monthly re-turn—a very complicated report, for a new beginer to make.

Sept. 19th.—With four days rations in haversacks embarked on a down train—going to Kentucky certain, this time.

Sept. 20th.—Arrived at Jackson at 10 A.M., and immediately left on the southern road for Meridian, where arrived, 12 night. Nothing but pine forests—on the roads.

Sept. 21st.—Had an excellent breakfast at the hotel. Our train stood on a switch until late in the evening, when we ran down below town and disembarked. Established camp on a nice grassy plot, im-mediately on the rail road. We are here waiting orders from Breck-inridge, whether to go via Mobile or Demopolis.

Sept. 22d.—This morning, Companies "A" and "C" stacked arms, stating their times was out and declaring the "C.S. Government" had no right to conscript them. Col. C[25]—Col. H. still being away wounded—had them all put under guard, Co. B. being detailed to guard them. This evening Col. H. came in camp on crutches, and talked to the "mutineers" awhile. They all returned to duty, being promised the War Department would be consulted, as to whether they could be held in service, or not. Got on cars in the evening, late, and remained on side-track all night.[26]

Sept. 23d.—Left Meridian at daylight, on new road being con-structed to Demopolis. The road being new, the train ran very slowly, taking nearly all day to run out to York station, the terminus of the road. Once the car in front of the Col's, ran off, and went

---

23. The injured man was probably Captain Ed S. Worthington, 4th Kentucky In-fantry. Thompson, p. 622, notes only that he was "disabled by an accident for active field duty."

24. Second Lieutenant Peter O'Connor, Company H, 9th Kentucky Infantry. Thompson, p. 848.

25. Lieutenant Colonel John W. Caldwell.

26. For full details on the mutiny of September 22 and the succeeding one on Oc-tober 8, 1862, see Davis, pp. 129–33.

bouncing over the ties. I looked out to see what was the matter, and saw the men, even in front of the car, jumping off. Expecting every moment our car would run off, we commenced "rolling out"—the Col. first, to show the balance how to jump; then followed the staff, not questioning rank. The car kept running over the ties for several hundred yards, before the train was stopped. Looking back, the road was lined with soldiers; some getting up, feeling their heads and limbs, to see that no bones were broken; others were still lying on the ground; and a crowd came following the train, some limping, some laughing. The car was soon put on the track, and we went on.

Went into camp near York station, 30 miles from Meridian. Are waiting for wagons to haul our camp equipage to Demopolis, 20 or 30 miles distant.

Sept. 24th.—Late in the evening loaded our baggage on the train, and after night cooked rations. We shall go the Mobile route.

Sept. 25th.—Train started early and we got to Meridian by noon. Our car was on the passenger train. The train on which the regiment was transported was delayed until nearly dark by engine running off the track.

Sept. 26th.—Left Meridian at 9 a.m. and on road all day, running to Mobile. At noon, a rain set in, and kept up all through the day and night. The road to Mobile, is through one interminable pine forest— almost a wilderness. When we got to the city—a little after dark—the train was put on a side-track. All the officers and men, nearly, imme- diately went out into the city—to "have a time." I preferred staying at home, and passed a very disagreeable night—the car leaking badly.

Sept. 27th.—A murky morning. "Old Trib." as the boys call Col. Trabue, tried to keep us all at the depot, but soon the whole brigade was scattered over the city. All bent on having a spree. I went down on the quay, first place, to see the bay. The fog was just lifting, and had a very pretty view. Feeling like breakfast, I stepped into an oys- ter saloon, and took a *few dozen* stewed. When I got back to the depot, I found drays and wagons ready to transport our baggage to the wharf. The rain again commenced pouring down, and kept up all the time we were moving. Our regiment embarked on an old cotton boat, the "Waverly"—the 4th and 6th, on a fine passenger steamer, the "R.B. Taney." We lay at the wharf all day, after we had em- barked. The day turned out beautiful. The boys kept coming aboard in squads, many in a condition, "how come you so." Just as the sun was disappearing "behind the western waters," the good steamer

"Waverly" cast loose, and steamed up the Alabama. Soon the "Taney" followed, and a race was inevitable. Our steam was down, and they soon past us, cheering and giving us "music on the waters," from brass bands, mingled with a screaming calliope. Company "H" of our regiment, being nearly all steamboatmen, took charge of affairs, and soon the "Waverly" mounted the waves like a "thing of life." It seemed every man in the regiment turned fireman, pro tempore. When we overtook the "Taney" she was turned across the channel to keep us from passing, but we ran around her and went on. The night was dark and misty.

Sept. 28th.—When morning came, our "antagonist" was nowhere to be seen. We stopped at a wood yard, and cooked two days rations. Just as we were getting through, the "Taney" passed us. We hurried on board, and soon left her behind again. Cloudy all day; but no rain fell.

Sept. 29th.—Clouds broke away at noon. The boys amused themselves by shooting at aligators lying out on the sand-bars and banks, sunning themselves. The scenery all up the river is monotonous. The banks are generally low, and the country, seen from the boat, not much improved: sometimes fine plantations could be seen skirting the river. Passed two towns to-day, Cahawba and Selma—the latter quite a place. Saw two iron-clads being built at Selma; and formidable looking craft, too.[27] Soon after passing Selma, darkness again "came over the waters."

Sept. 30th.—At noon arrived at Montgomery, having traveled 450 miles by water. Our baggage was moved to the depot by 3 P.M. and we took train for West Point, Ga. I did not have time to look over Montgomery much. The train sped away between 3 and 4 p.m., and until dark set in, we were rushing through pine forests. Goodness! shall we ever get out of these pines? Took supper at the Taladega Junction. Arrived at West Point, midnight.

Oct. 1st.—Changed cars for Atlanta at 8 A.M. Until 2 P.M., reaching Atlanta. At La Grange, Newman, and other towns, a throng of ladies at the depots, to give us a cheer. By the time we got to Atlanta, the cars were piled up with boquets. In Atlanta, all the people were scared, having heard that Breckinridge's "wild Kentuckians", were coming through. At 7 P.M. where led off on the Western & Atlantic Road. Having heard we were coming, the Kentucky refugees

---

27. The ironclads Jackman saw were probably the *Tuscaloosa* and the *Huntsville*, both of which later saw service at Mobile.

at Marietta were at the depot to see us. I was asleep at the time, and
did not see any of the "bright eyes" from the "promised land."

Oct. 2d.—At Dalton by daylight. Here Gen'l Breckinridge came in
our car for the balance of the trip. At 10 a.m., left on the Ga. and
East Tenn. road for Knoxville. At every station the train stopped, the
people found out that Breckinridge was on board, and would crowd
around the car to see him. Often he was requested to speak, but he
always declined. Up in East Tennessee—out of the pines at last! The
country begins to look natural—see stacks of grain, fields of heavy
corn, fat cattle, hogs, etc. Once a crowd came to see the General,
who was out at the time, and Dr. P., our surgeon, was pointed out to
them as the General, and they went off as well satisfied as if they had
seen the *rara avis* sure enough. Got to Knoxville at 10 P.M., Slept in
the cars all night.

Oct. 3d.—Went into camp a short distance from town. While here,
we lived off the "fat of the land." We had very good rations issued to
us, and there was a plentiful and cheap market at hand. Was very
busy in the office all the time, making reports, and recording orders,
which had gotten behind before I came into the office. The troops
were being thoroughly organized and equipped, for a march into
Kentucky. While this was going on the time of some of the 6th Ky.
expired, and they refused to do duty longer. Genl. B. came out, and
had the brigade drawn up about him. He made a little speech to the
boys, giving all a little raking over for being so wild, and having made
too free with other folks' property, during the late trip; and then
he addressed himself to our boys that had stacked arms at Meridian.
He told them he was surprised at their having acted so. That, though
he had since been told, the action was to raise the question whether
the government had a right to hold them in the service or not,
which, he said, would take some of the edge off the crime—yet, if he
had been there, he would have had either unconditional surrender,
or unconditional mutiny. He then said that as an investigation had
been promised them, he would see that they received an answer
from the War Department. He wound up by giving the "mutineers,"
in the 6th fifteen minutes to return to duty, and they all did so, before the time expired.[28]

Our company having heard Bragg's Army was at Bardstown, all in a
glee, thinking they would soon be home. Alas! they knew not then

---

28. See note 26.

how many hard marches were before them—how many battles had to
be fought, and yet, never march into Kentucky. In ten or twelve
days, every thing was put in order for a long march. The greatest
trouble was in getting transportation.

Oct. 15th.—All things being ready, broke up camp, and marched
12 miles towards Cumberland Gap. All marched with a buoyant step.
There was no straggling, and the column kept well closed up. Col.
Hanson, in command of brigade.[29] We went into camp before sun
down and pitched our tents in regular order. We are going to Kentucky in grand style.

Oct. 16th.—Had reveille early and cooked breakfast. I had to make
out Morning Report, which kept me busy. Marched over a rough
road to-day, the country being hilly. Far ahead of us, can see the
mountains, which look like a blue cloud rising above the horizon.
Having beautiful Autumn days—Indian summer. Marched 15 miles,
passed through Maynardsville and a few miles beyond, camped in an
old clover field. Writing until late.

Oct. 17th.—When the column got fairly out on the road, this
morning, a courier came dashing up to Gen'l Breckinridge, and handed
him a despatch. We were ordered back, and pitched our tents on old
grounds. Various rumors are afloat about camp, as to the cause of our
delay. Some say that Bragg has been whipped; and is retreating from
Kentucky; others say he has captured a large lot of supplies and is
sending a large wagon train through the Gap, that we shall have to
wait until it passes: and various other rumors are going the rounds.

Oct. 19th.—Early, struck tents, and with "heads all lowly bend-
ing," marched 15 miles towards Knoxville. Camped where we did,
the first night out. Going to Kentucky "played out." The boys not as
cheerful to-day, as when going on the road the other way. They did
not keep up so well.

Oct. 20th.—Marched to Knoxville, and camped on old grounds.
Saw many refugees coming out from Kentucky.

Oct. 21st.—Moved by rail to Chattanooga. Had to cross a very
high bridge over the Tennessee. Arrived at Chattanooga after night.

---

29. Colonel Roger W. Hanson, captured at Fort Donelson, had been released from
prison and returned to take command of the brigade, as senior colonel, when the brigade reached Knoxville on October 3. Davis, p. 127.

It was also upon arriving at Knoxville that Colonel Hunt and the men of his 5th
Kentucky learned the news that Richmond had resolved the confusion of the two
5th Kentucky regiments by redesignating Jackman's unit the 9th Kentucky Infantry.
Thompson, p. 45.

Oct. 22d.—Left Chattanooga in the forenoon, and got off the train near Shell Mound. Camped regularly on the side of the road. The Tennessee "rolls her crystal waters" in sight of camp. The mountain scenery about us is grand—picturesque. Shell Mound is nothing more than a station on the Nashville and Chattanooga railroad, 16 miles distant from the latter place.

Oct. 25th.—In the evening, struck tents, and loaded our baggage on the train to be run down to the river, opposite Bridge Port. We then marched down on the rail road, being 5 miles. Dark was setting in when we unloaded our baggage on the side of the rail-road, and bivouacked among the drifts. Looking like rain, we pitched our tent—and well we did as, for when morning came, the ground was covered with snow. A very sudden change, yesterday being too hot for comfortable marching.

Oct. 26th.—The Tennessee is here divided by an island, nearly half a mile in width, and a bridge spans each arm of the river, the island being the center pier. The old bridges were burned during last summer, and the new ones, now up, are not far enough advanced for trains to cross—Whew! Wintery this morning, and had to carry all of our baggage 200 yards to the landing. Here a company, at a time, got on board of a small steam boat, and ferried over to the island—then lugged across to another boat, and was put over on the Bridge Port side. By 3 P.M. our regiment was packed away in a train of cars like sardines. I believe we never were before as crowded on a train. I stood up nearly all the time the train having left at 4 P.M., and running all night.[30]

Oct. 27th.—About noon arrived at Murfreesboro, and the first man I saw was Bro. W.[31] who was in company with "Capt." G.—Took dinner with them.—

In the evening established camp half a mile from town, on the Shelbyville pike. Camped nearly on the same grounds we occupied on retreat from Kentucky.

---

30. On October 26, 1862, Breckinridge officially rejoined the 2d Kentucky, released from prison, and the 6th Kentucky, from Preston's brigade, with the 4th and 9th regiments and Cobb's battery, essentially reconstituting the original First Kentucky Brigade. Thus, with occasional alterations, including the addition of the official 5th Kentucky on November 3, 1863, the brigade would remain for the balance of the war. Thompson, p. 109; Davis, pp. 137, 194.

31. William Jackman.

•4•

Trying His Hand in
a Fight: Murfreesboro

The Battle of Murfreesboro, or Stones River, would always remain one of the bitterest memories for the Kentuckians. In the terrible days of fighting, they took fearful losses, especially on January 2, 1863, when Bragg sent Breckinridge's command into an ill-advised charge that saw Hanson mortally wounded and hundreds of the brigade killed or wounded. So devastated was the brigade that a distraught Breckinridge wept before them and called them "my poor orphans," using, for perhaps the first time, the name by which they are now most remembered. For years afterward an antipathy existed between them and Bragg, who spent the next several months feuding with Breckinridge.

Recovered from his Baton Rouge wound, Helm, now a brigadier, reassumed command from the slain Hanson, and the brigade went into the best winter quarters it enjoyed during the war, passing its time with theatricals and balls and drill competitions. Then on May 24 they were sent off to Vicksburg again, this time to try to avert the river city's capture by U. S. Grant. They did not reach Vicksburg in time, and after its surrender they withdrew to Jackson, Mississippi, as part of an army led by General Joseph E. Johnston. There they tried unsuccessfully to hold the city against William T. Sherman. Forced to withdraw, they moved into the interior to Camp Hurricane for another miserable Deep South summer.

Now commenced a long siege of monotonous camp life. However, I was kept busy writing all the time, and did not have an opportunity of watching how the heavy hours went by. The boys too, were kept pretty busy drilling and standing guard. Col. Hanson, soon after promoted to brigadier general, now took command of the brigade, and had every thing done up in military order. He was the best disciplinarian we ever had. The brigade was all under the same guard line, and at dress parade, the whole brigade would be in perfect line of battle, on the color-line. Guard duty had to be done to the letter. "Old Roger," as we called the General—Most of his own regiment called him "Flintlock"—was going the rounds at all hours of the night, to see that all was well. The boys had many adventures with him.[1]

We lived well all the time we were encamped at Murfreesboro. Good rations were issued us, and we always could buy butter, chickens, eggs, turkeys, sweet potatoes, apples, etc., from the country people at the old rates, paying "confederate."

Soon after coming to Murfreesboro, two fresh companies were added to the reg't—one commanded by Capt. Jo. Desha,[2] raised about Cynthiana, Ky., and the other by Lt. Gains,[3] raised about Frankfort. Our reg't was then very large; but two Tennessee companies were transferred from it, and left it about the usual size.

Late in the fall, when the weather got cool, the boys built brick chimneys to their tents, which made them quite comfortable.

We had an army stove in the office, made of sheet iron. By keeping it full of wood all the time, our tent was kept very warm and cozy.

Nov. 4th.—Brigade marched with three days rations in haversacks towards Nashville. The camp was left standing. Am left behind making Monthly Return and so on. Col. Hunt having requested me to sleep in his tent at night, I did so, sleeping magnificently in the Col's feather-bed.

The brigade returned to camp the next day, or the day after, I have forgotten which. The movement was feint on Nashville, going within five miles of the city. Morgan came into Edgefield, opposite the city, at the same time.

---

1. The often irascible Hanson had several nicknames. He was also known as "Bench-leg," thanks to a stiff leg due to a prewar dueling wound. Davis, p. 52.

2. Joseph Desha commanded Company I of the 9th Kentucky. Thompson, p. 729.

3. Captain J. T. Gaines and his company were later reassigned in May 1863 as Company K, 5th Kentucky. Thompson, pp. 497, 737.

Dec. 5th.—Early the brigade fell in, equipped for a campaign, and marched away, leaving the camp standing. I was left behind again. A heavy snow storm was passing, and soon the gray column was lost to view in the whirling snow. The brigade marched 18 miles, and bivouacked at Beard's Mills. Here, the next day, 6th, at 2 P.M., a force was organized for the expedition to Hartsville, composed of the 9th and 2d Ky. infantry, under Col. Hunt, and two of Morgan's regiments of cavalry. The whole force was commanded by Morgan. A section of Cobb's battery was also along. The expedition got to the Cumberland river, 25 miles, by midnight, and the infantry immediately commenced crossing over in an old leaky ferry-flat which had to be kept afloat by constant bailing. The cavalry, and I believe the artillery, forded the river.

Dec. 7th.—By daylight, all were over, and the column pushed on to the camps, yet five miles off. The enemy was attacked at sun-rise, and an engagement of three fourths of an hour, caused him to surrender his whole force, 2000 strong. By noon the confederates were back across the river—the rear being shelled some, by the Federal reinforcements coming up—and by 9 P.M., were back at Beard's Mills with the balance of the brigade. On the evening of the 8th, all returned to camp well loaded down with booty. Had three stands of colors—the prisoners were left in town.[4]

Dec. 13th.—"Jeff" reviewing the troops. First reviewed our brigade, and was well pleased with the "orphans." They conducted themselves "every inch the soldier." They passed in review, marching perfectly. Hanson was made brigadier general on the spot. First time I ever saw "old Jeff."[5]

From that time, nothing of interest going on. I was kept pretty busy all of the time, making reports and recording orders—large number coming in daily.

---

4. Jackman's account of Hartsville is obviously hearsay since he did not accompany the brigade on the expedition. In fact, 1,834 Federals surrendered after the brief engagement, in which they had put up a poor showing. Davis, pp. 143–46.

5. "Jeff," of course, is President Jefferson Davis, who visited the Army of Tennessee in December 1862. No other evidence indicates that he promoted Hanson to brigadier "on the spot," as Jackman says, but Hanson's appointment did officially date from December 13, 1862. Erza J. Warner, *Generals in Gray* (Baton Rouge, La.: Louisiana State University Press, 1959), p. 124.

Dec. 28th.—This morning the brigade moved out on Stone River. The camp is left standing. Adjt. C.[6] ordered me to stay with the office. He seems to have a presentiment something is going to happen to him. Left word with me for Maj. W.,[7] who is away on special duty. A beautiful sunny day, and a stream of glittering bayonets has been pouring through town all day long—troops marching out to their respective positions in the line-of-battle. In the evening, a detail came from the regiment, and struck tents, loaded the wagons. While thus occupied, Col. H. came into camp, having started away the evening before on a leave of absence, but had now come back to participate in the battle. Feeling like I would have some adventure, as well as the other boys, I asked the Col. to let me go with the regiment. He seldom refuses a fellow the privilege of "trying his hand in a fight", and told me to come out, after seeing that every thing was packed away in the wagon properly. One of our company had been left in camp, too sick to walk, and, after dark, went to the College hospital to get him admitted, which I did after a good deal of talk. Came back, and sent him away on horseback. The wagon train moved out on the Manchester pike about 9 P.M. Looked desolate enough about the old camp. The numbers of brick chimneys left standing alone, made it appear a city had been destroyed on the spot. Billie A.,[8] who was sick, and going out with me, & I concluded to stay there until morning. We tried to sleep, but without much success, as the wagon trains were rumbling and roaring over the pike all night, the teamsters popping their whips and yelling.

Monday Dec. 29th.—When morning came, we got up, shook off the drowsiness, ate our breakfast, then started for the regiment, lying in line of battle. The morning was beautiful, being the commencement of one of those lovely Indian summer days, which sometimes, come, even in the winter season, down south. Though the day was beautiful, *a storm was brewing.* The deep resonance of cannon came rolling over the hills from towards Nashville, and we could *sniff saltpeter in the air.* Two miles from town, came up with the regiment, the boys lying lazily about on a rocky hill, waiting the coming of

---

6. First Lieutenant Henry Curd of Company H, 9th Kentucky. His premonition, unless Jackman invented it as an after-the-fact embellishment, turned out to be correct. Thompson, p. 848.

7. Major John C. Wickliffe was away collecting absentees. Thompson, p. 448.

8. William Ambrose, Company B, 9th Kentucky. Thompson, p. 816.

events. A wagon came out with rations and cooking utensils, and we
cooked rations. The thunder of cannon kept coming nearer. As the
gloom of evening set in, a large brick mansion (Cowan's house) across
the river from us, and in front of Withers'[9] division, was set on fire,
to be burned out of the way, and high up leaped the flames, mingled
with an inky column of smoke, which pierced the very heavens.
Gloomy sight, at such a time as this. Soon after, our cavalry, which
had been falling back in front of the Federal Army, burst out of the
cedars in front of Withers, and also came dashing back from our side
of the river. We immediately fell in, and advanced, in line of battle,
over a rocky ravine and through an old field, where the weeds were
up to our shoulders, and so thick we could hardly march. The
evening was warm, and I had a heavy overcoat on, which with
tugging through the weeds, caused me to nearly suffocate. I pulld
it off once, with the intention of abandoning it, but again picked it
up, and buckled it under my belt. Well I did so, for afterwards, it
came in good place. We halted and sent forward Co. D, as skirmishers. They moved forward, to a corn field, and were soon engaged.
Lt. B.,[10] in command, being wounded, the field named, being on a
hill, which, if taken possession of by the enemy, would have been
disastrous to us, for it was the key to our position: I don't know
why we were not ordered to take position on this hill in the beginning. We moved forward to support our skirmishers, and lay
down just under the crest of the hill. Cobb's battery was placed in
position on top. Darkness had now come on. The enemy advanced,
and drove our skirmishers in. They fired pretty briskly for a time,
making the cornstalks rattle about us. In the darkness, the Federal
skirmish-line came right up among the battery, which was being un-
limbered a little in advance of us. One of the "Feds" hallowed out,
"Boys here is a cannon, let us get away from here," and they all
skedaddled. Two of our regiments then advanced, and the Federal
force, what-ever it was, withdrew over the river. A strong skirmish
line was then established on the margin of the rivers and the brigade
fell back into the old weed-fields, where they slept on their arms. I
went back to the rocky-hill, to stay by a fire. About midnight a rain

---

9. Brigadier General Jones M. Withers.
10. First Lieutenant Andrew J. Beale, Company D, 9th Kentucky. Thompson, p.
830.

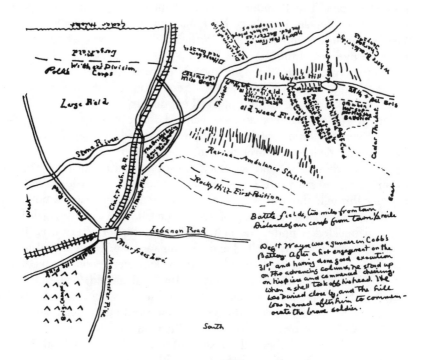

Map 1

rain set in, and I adjourned to a neighboring corn-crib, and slept in the shucks.[11]

Dec. 30th.—A murky morning—misting rain. Started for the regiment, and found it had moved. I then went back to where Billie A. was having some coffee made by his boy—Billie was not able to be with the regiment, but was on the field. Stayed with him until the afternoon when I went to the regiment. The enemy shelling our lines during the day. Our army kept quiet. We did see a little fight-

---

11. The eminence Jackman speaks of is Wayne's Hill, and the Federals who came nearly up to Cobb's guns were men of Colonel Abel Streight's 51st Indiana Infantry. William R. Hartpence, *History of the Fifty-First Indiana Veteran Volunteer Infantry* (Harrison, Ohio: Robert Clark Co., 1894), pp. 104–6.

ing in front of Withers. We had a tent—fly, which we put up temporarily to shield us from the rain. Sometimes the shells would make us seek shelter behind a big rock. In the afternoon, the rain having slacked up, I sought out the regiment, which I found lying about in a cedar thicket, grumbling at the weather. Sometimes, too, shells would come tearing through the cedars, making a fellow feel uncomfortable. At last, night came on, and we moved back into the ravine, in rear of the line, near where I found them on first coming out and near where Billie and I had been all day. Here the boys had fires— Rain ceased at dark. I slept with Billie A. under our fly.

Wed. Dec. 31st.—The sun came up clear. The regiment had moved off before I waked up. Had breakfast. The ambulances and caisons are sheltered in our ravine. Just as the sun was coming up I heard a yelling over towards Withers' division, and ran up on the hill to see the cause. That division was charging across a big field in perfect line of battle, the men yelling and cheering. Soon tho the Federal batteries opened on them, then the musketry, and I could see his men falling. Presently they opened fire, and the line was obscured in smoke. This was, I believe, the grandest scene I ever witnessed, in the military line. I stood a moment watching the battle, and a stray shell came near cutting me down. Thinking the ball had now opened in earnest, I "buckled on my armor", and started for the regiment. One of the boys was with me. We had to pass over a long field in the rear of a battery, which was then being subject to a heavy fire. First, a shell would tear up the ground in front of us; then we would go a little slow; then a ball would plow up the ground in rear of us; then we would quicken our pace. When we got to the regiment, it was falling in to march out in rear of the battery, which was composed of twelve guns and on the hill where we skirmished the first evening. As soon as the regiment got to the proper place, a short distance from the guns, ordered to lie down. Our battery, or batteries, for there were three parked together, opened fire on the advancing columns, and the Federal guns replied, firing over the heads of their troops. I believe, there were 38 cannon playing on us at once. The hill protected us a little, yet I saw from my position, on the extreme left of the regiment, numbers of cannon balls strike just in front of the line, and skip over. We were not behind the battery more than five minutes, for seeing the numbers that were being hurt, Gen'l Hanson had the regiment moved off a little to the right, out of range. In this, we lost about 20 or 30 wounded, but luckily no one killed. We did not move again during the day. Our company went to get in the trenches, by the guns, in the evening, but the order was countermanded, and it came back. Just before sundown, a cannon ball passed through Adjt. C. killing him instantly. I had just left his side, having been to him to get some tobacco. The day was cool, though the sun shown out all the time—cold wind from the North. Lying on the cold ground a good deal during the day, was chilled, and when darkness put a stop to the stirring scenes, I went back to the ambulance station, to get by the fire. Dr. B[12] gave me a "drink", and we spread down blankets together. Slept well.

Thur. Jany. 1st, 1863.—All quiet to-day. Both armies seem to be taking a "blowing spell," after the hard fighting yesterday. Turned my gun over to one of the infirmary corps, they having to take arms.—[13]

Friday Jany 2d.—Raining in the morning. Back at the ambulance train nearly all the time. All quiet until about 3 P.M., when Bragg ordered Breckinridges division to charge *over Stone River,* at Rosecranz'[14] army! All the brigade went into the charge, save our regiment, which was left to support the batteries, and hold the hill, heretofore mentioned. The rain stopped just before the charge was made. Hanson killed.—[15]

Jany 3d.—Rain pouring down all day long. At the regiment part of the time, helping dig in the entrenchment. Late in the evening, having "got wind" that the army was going [to] fall back that night, I went into town to see Bro. W. at Dr. S's.[16] Soon after getting in town, the rain came down in torrents, and continued all night long. Went to the Medical Purveyor's office, and there found Bro. W., Dr. S., and Dr. P.,[17] medical director of division. They had been on the field and had gotten things nice to eat and still had some on hand.

---

12. Dr. Walter J. Byrne, surgeon of the 9th Kentucky. Thompson, p. 299.

13. Jackman, still officially detailed as adjutant's clerk, was not required to bear arms, and had been doing so only voluntarily.

14. Major General William S. Rosecrans.

15. It is ironic that Jackman says so little about the assault of January 2, 1862, at Stones River, for it was one of the two or three most memorable actions his brigade participated in. Considering the fact that his regiment did not participate, it is probable that this brief entry was written at the time and not subsequently elaborated. As for Hanson, an artillery fuse from a exploding shell struck and severed the femoral artery in his left knee. He died on January 4. Davis, pp. 157, 161.

16. William A. Jackman and Dr. Preston B. Scott, brigade surgeon. Thompson, p. 303.

17. Dr. John E. Pendleton, medical director of Breckinridge's division. Thompson, p. 299.

Not having eaten any thing but "dough" for a week, I enjoyed a good supper. Wrote home, giving the letter to Dr. P. to mail, as he was to be left with the wounded. Troops marching back, through town all night. Slept with Bro. W., before a huge fire in the office.

Jany 4th.—Up before daylight: The Dr. having a spare horse, I was to ride. We mounted just at daylight, and rode off through a pelting rain. All had left before the dawn. We overtook our regiment 5 miles from town, on the Manchester pike, acting as rear guard. Being mounted, Col. H. sent me ahead to turn back an ordnance wagon. The road was a perfect "loblolly", and in riding by the infantry, sometimes I would splatter mud on them, and often expected to be bayonetted. In the after part of the day the sun came out hot. Evening came up with the wagon train, camped near Manchester. Not having been on horseback for so long, this ride of 30 miles tired me almost as much as if I had walked.

Jany. 5th.—The wagon train started on for Tullahoma. Got five, or 6 miles on the road, and ordered back to Manchester, where arrived after dark. Raining after night. Slept with Bro. W. on a pile of hospital comforts, which caught fire and could hardly be put out.

Jany. 6th.—In the morning the regiment came up. The train being again ordered towards Tullahoma, I kept with it on "my horse." When we got as far as we did before, the wagons of our regiment were ordered back to Manchester. Being on horseback I didn't care much for these "notionate" movements. Just after dark we found the regiment in camp near town. I dismounted and resigned my steed to the Dr. That night my Mess did not put up the tent—we slept on it. Late at night I waked up with something heavy on my face. I found it to be an old gander, quietly roosting on my head, which some of the boys had brought into camp—I presume he saw that I had no feathers under my head, and concluded to put some on top, instead of underneath. I thanked him, by flinging him against a stump, hardby.

Now commences another long siege of inaction. Nothing much to vary one day from another—a routine of camp duty, from one weeks end to another. I made no entries in my Journal during the time we encamped at Manchester, from Jany 6th, to April 23d.

Manchester, the County-town of Coffin, is a small place on the branch rail road running to McMinnville. At the time we sojourned in its vicinity, the town was very much torn up, both armies having had a turn at the place. The boys, however, found enough society to keep up amusement, and all the winter, were flirting with the young

ladies. Balls were frequent. I attended two—one at a hotel in town—
the other, at an unfinished paper mill below town, on Duck river.
When the latter came off, a rain poured down all night, so no one
could go home. At this ball, Gus M. & Co.,[18] played Bombastes Fu-
rioso, a stage having been arranged for the purpose. The boys would
defray all expenses, in getting refreshments etc. When they would go
out to invite the girls, the old dames would be informed an abundance of *pure coffee* would be on hand, which all objections to their
"girls" going to the ball would cease—"You may look for *me* and my
'gals' to be thar, shore." The boys knew the proper cord to touch, to
bring the "gals." The "gals" would dance, and the old ladies would
sip coffee.

The brigade, soon after coming to Manchester, was placed under
command of Brig. Gen'l Ben Harden Helm,[19] *vice* Brig. Gen'l Roger
W. Hanson, killed at Murfreesboro. The boys had a good deal of drilling to do. The brigade at different times was drilled and reviewed in
the presence of Gen'ls Breckinridge, Hardee[20] and J. E. Johnston.[21]
They all pronounced them the best drilled troops in the army.

Our regiment was stationed alone, for several weeks at Manchester, before the balance of the brigade came up from Tullahoma. The
boys conducted themselves in such a manner that they won the es-
teem of the people. They thought the 9th Ky. was the best regiment in the army. When the other regiments came up, a great many
depredations were committed, that is, hogs killed and so on, but
none of the people laid any blame on the 9th. If our boys ever did do

---

18. The theatrical and ball were held February 24, 1863, apparently the brainchild
of Augustus J. Moore of Company B, 9th Kentucky. Thompson, p. 821; Davis, p. 169;
Squire Helm Bush diary, February 24, 1863, Hardin County Historical Society, Elizabethtown, Kentucky.

Johnny Green described one of the incidents of calling upon young ladies in his own
diary/memoir:

Upon the occasion of my next call I took John Jackman with me to entertain one
sister while I tried to gain favor of Miss Sukey's [Miss Sukey Hickerson] good graces.
We had come away from camp without leave & the hour for roll call was near. We
had nearly a mile to go to camp, a sleet had set in & we had to cross the creek on a
log incased in a sheet of ice. So hurried was our pace that when I got half way across
the creek I slipped off & went cosouze in the water up to my waist. This made Jack
so nervous that he sat straddle of the log & cooned it across. After all we missed roll
call & had to serve an extra term of guard duty for it. (Kirwan, p. 71)

19. General Ben Hardin Helm had recovered from his Baton Rouge wound and,
being next senior, assumed command after Hanson's death.

20. Lieutenant General William J. Hardee.

21. General Joseph E. Johnston.

such things, which is highly probable, all went to the credit of the other regiments.

There was church every night in town, for several weeks before we marched, chaplains generally officiating.

A night or two before we moved from Manchester, the brigade marched towards McMinnville, to apprehend a *cavalry raid.* The rain was hitting down, and the night as dark as Erebus. Saw nothing of the enemy. I was not along.

April 23d.—Broke up camp at Manchester & marched to Beech Grove, 12 miles toward Murfreesboro. Camped in a clover field. The hills about here remind me of Kentucky. They are covered with such pastures and beautiful groves of beech trees, which are now leaving-out. Spring-time is again coming over the hills with "gayety and song." The brigade is commanded temporarily by Col. H., Gen'l Helm being in command of ours and Brown's[22] brigade. Beech Grove, in other days, had a country grocery and post office: there is a nice church, which is still used as a place of worship.

April 25th.—Moved camp two miles down the creek, and pitched our tents on a ridge, in a grove of beech trees. Beautiful prospect from camp—can see for miles over gentle undulating fields and green pastures on the one hand—on the other, is stern mountain scenery. The yeomen are at work. The merry whistles which the farmer boy sends up from the field does not accord with our shrill fifes—neither do our occupations. This morning ordered to be ready to march at day-light to-morrow morning.

April 26th.—Last night the order to move was countermanded.— Monotonous in camp.

May 1st.—Moved to Jacob's store, mile and half, on the pike, south end Hoover's Gap.

May 2d.—Our regiment thrown forward as advanced infantry, and camped one mile in the Gap. Our camp is in a pleasant place. On either side of the pike, are hills mountain high. Our division is to defend this place.

May 5th.—Climbed a high hill near camp, and could see Murfreesboro, 17 miles off; also the smoke rising from the camps of the "Army of the Cumberland," about the place. Far beyond, could see the blue hills bordering the Cumberland river. I remained nearly all day, admiring the grand scenery about me.

---

22. John C. Brown.

May 19th.—Monotonous about camp until this morning, when the regiment went 2 miles to the front on picket. I went to brigade Hd.Qrs. with papers, and while there, witnessed a trial drill between the 6th Ky. and 16th La. regiment, Adam's[23] brigade, which took place in a field close by. Looked like "fair times." Carriages were drawn up all about the field, which had brought ladies to witness the grand military turnout. Gen'ls Hardee, Breckinridge, H. Marshall,[24] Palmer,[25] Brown, Adams, and Helm, present—Palmer and Brown, Judges. Both regiments drilled admirably. The Judges decided in favor of the 6th Ky. All the regiments in Adam's and Helm's brigades are to drill against each other, coming in according to rank of Colonels commanding, beginning at oldest; then the judges will select the best drilled regiment in each brigade, and let them have a trial drill. After this is over a brigade drilling match will come off. The challenge came from Gen'l Adams. His brigade is in Breckinridge's division.

May 20th.—Witnessed the trial drill between the 13th La. Reg't— their crack regiment—and 2d Ky Reg't. Both regiments drilled splendidly. I believe the judges again decided in favor of the Kentuckians. The regiment came in off picket at 7 P.M.

May 21st.—Hard to decide which best drilling the 4th Ky., or the 19th La.—that is, in my mind—but believe the judges decided in favor of the 4th.

May 22d.—This was the day for our regiment to drill against the 32d Ala. Reg't, Adam's brigade, but the Col. of the Ala. regiment being sick, the drill did not come off. While the boys were cooking dinner, the regiment ordered to the front immediately. A few minutes later, the brigade passed going to the front. All back by middle afternoon—false alarm.

May 23d.—Order came after night to cook rations, preparatory to a move the next morning.

May 24th.—Had reveille early, loaded baggage and moved out. Very hot day, and we had to march 12 miles to Wartrace, on the Nashville and Chattanooga railroad, where we arrived shortly after 12 N., and bivouacked near the town, in a wood. All the boys suspected that the brigade was ordered to Mississippi, and were grumbling a great deal, not liking to make another summer campaign in

23. Daniel W. Adams.
24. Humphrey Marshall of Kentucky.
25. Joseph B. Palmer.

that state. Shortly after we stacked arms, Gen'l Breckinridge sent around an order for all the brigade to assemble at brigade Hd. Qrs. at a given signal—that he wished to speak to the "boys." Many said that if the brigade was ordered to reinforce Johnston,[26] and if left with them to vote whether to stay or go, they would vote to stay in Tennessee. We fell in without arms, and the regiments were drawn up about the Gen'l. He got up on a stump, and commenced by telling them that he had received orders from Gen'l Bragg to report at Wartrace with all of his division, save that portion composed of Tennessee troops, and hold himself in readiness to move on the cars. He said that he was not to receive further orders until he reached Atlanta, but that he had a pretty good idea where they were going, and that he supposed the boys could also guess at their destination. He said that knowing they would object to making a campaign in a climate so deleterious to health, especially in the summer season, he had, through Gen'l Hardee, sent a communication to Gen'l Bragg requesting that the Kentucky troops of his division be also permitted to remain with the army of Tennessee and Mississippi troops be given him instead, who would be glad to get back to their native state. He said that in reply to this communication, Gen'l Bragg left it to his (Breckinridge's) option, whether the Ky. troops would go or stay. This, he said, had left him in a dilemma, and that he intended to leave the question with them to decide. Bragg and Breckinridge had been at "logger-heads" since the battle of Murfreesboro; and the boys felt that if they did not vote to follow their Maj. Gen'l, outsiders would think they also condemned him as well as Bragg: so when the vote was put, they not only held up their right hands, to a man, but cheered loudly. The Gen'l then thanked them in a little, but eloquent speech. He is the most eloquent speaker I ever heard—Bivouacked for the night where we first stopped.

May 25th.—At 6 P.M. all of our regiment got on the train, (save one or two companies,) on which the 6th Ky. was "stored." Col. C, and the col. of the 6th,[27] had to take a car in partnership, and we were very much crowded. The train ran away with the engineer, while coming down the mountain, this side the Tunnel. The grade is steep and 7 miles long, and we ran the 7 miles in *4 minutes and a*

---

26. Joseph E. Johnston had been ordered to assemble an army to move to the relief of the beseiged garrison at Vicksburg.

27. Colonel John W. Caldwell, 9th Kentucky, and Colonel Joseph H. Lewis, 6th Kentucky. Thompson, p. 742.

half. I was sitting on a camp stool in the center of the car and could hardly keep my seat. The moon was just sinking behind the mountains, and as I watched it, as it were, skipping from crag to crag, I thought farewell "old moon." I'll never see you again! We thought every moment the car would be dashed in pieces against the rocks, or be pitched off some of the cliffs and ground into dust. At last the train was stopped, and word came forward that the hindmost car, on which was company "C", had smashed up, or was missing at least. We all expected to find the last men killed, or badly hurt, and our surgeons started back to find them. I went back also. The car flew to pieces just as the train was at the bottom of the grade. No two pieces of it were left together; but fortunately, though some of the boys were hurt, not a man was killed, or a limb broken. One little fellow, that was on top of the car, was thrown clear over the telegraph wire, into a bramble of briars, receiving no worse injury than being "powerfully" scratched.

May 26th.—Arrived at Chattanooga at 8 A.M.

May 27th.—Arrived at Atlanta 5 A.M., and left for West Point at 8 A.M.—arrived at W.P. 6 P.M.

May 28th.—The regiment left at 10 A.M. on a train of flat cars. Dr. B. and I, *with a barrel of whisky in charge,* left at 1 P.M., on passenger train. Rain commenced pouring down about 11 A.M. and continued until next morning. Our train passed the regiment just before we got to Montgomery, and the boys looked like drowned rats. At the depot, the whiskey was issued out by buckets-full. Though dark as pitch and raining, we had to move on board the R.B. Taney. I slept on a chair, in the cabin, the remainder of the night.

May 29th.—Left the Montgomery wharf at daylight, and arrived at Selma 5 P.M.. Immediately disembarked and moved our baggage to the rail road, and at 8 P.M. were whirled off towards Demopolis. A passenger car was attached to the train, on which our regiment was being transported, for Gen'l Helm and Col. C. I "quished" myself on a cushioned seat and slept until we got to D. at 2 A.M. I thus missed the good things the people had at the stations, for the boys to eat.

May 30th.—Before daylight, commenced moving on board a small steamer, on the Tom Big Bee, and at sun-rise we dropped down the river 3 miles, when we disembarked, again meeting with rail road connection. When the road is completed a bridge will save all this trouble. At 11 A.M. the train moved off for Meridian, where we arrived at 5 P.M. Laid over on a switch for daylight.

May 31st.—At 7 A.M., train moved off for Jackson. In the evening, got off the train 6 miles from Jackson, the road having been torn up by the Federals that far out from the city, and went into camp. Suffered greatly for water.

June 3d.—Moved camp near the city, in an old field east of town, on the margin of a small lake, and not very far from Pearl river. The sun had full play upon us, but this was more healthy than camping in the woods. In the evening walked through the city, which presented quite a desolate appearance, a great deal of it having been lately burned down by Gen'l Grant's army. This improved the feelings of the inhabitants, though, towards the "Rebels," for now they bring water out on the streets for the soldiers marching through, when before, they would refuse a Rebel soldier a drink from their cisterns, or wells.

Now commences a month of monotonous camp life. When we started for Miss., we thought we would jump off the cars, and start immediately for the relief of Vicksburg. Our delay was caused for want of field transportation, and artillery horses. Our division remained camped about Jackson—Loring's, Walker's and Frenche's,[28] about Canton. The weather kept very hot all the time. We had a good place to bathe, in Pearl river. The boys caught a great many fish out of the lake and river. One way of catching them was rather novel: Two men would go into the lake, when the water was not very deep, and hold a blanket spread out, down close to the water, then others would commence lashing the water about, making it muddy, and the fish would commence skipping above the surface of the lake, and fall on the blanket, thus being caught by hundreds—I remained in camp all the time, seldom even going to the city. The cannonading was kept up steadily at Vicksburg, and the thunder of the guns could be easily heard at Jackson a distance of 40 miles. Sometimes the firing would be kept up day and night—other days would be perfectly quiet.

I made the following notes during month:

June 7th.—Regiment went out on the Clinton road to do picket duty.—*9th.*—Was waked up by the fire-bells in the city, and on opening my eyes, saw that the light of a fire was shining into the office—the walls of the tent being up—making it light as day. Could see the Bowman House, a large hotel near the Capitol, wrapped in flames, which roared not a little in the stillness of the night. Heavy cannonading all night at Vicksburg.—*16th.*—Regiment went on

28. William W. Loring, William H. T. Walker, and Samuel G. French.

picket to remain 48 hours. All quiet until 20th, when there was very heavy cannonading at Vicksburg.—*23d.*—At night the cannon roared at Vicksburg and continued all day the 24th—the heaviest firing heard yet.—*28th.*—Attended the Baptist church in Jackson—slim congregation. *June 30th.*—received marching orders. No cannonading since the 24th., at Vicksburg.

July 1st.—Have marched to-day 14 miles. Bivouacking 2 miles west of Clinton. The hotest march we have ever made. Many soldiers tumbled down in the road from sun-stroke. Water was very scarce. I had nothing to carry, but in helping the other boys along, wore myself out.

July 2d.—Reveille at 2 A.M. Had scarcely a wink of sleep last night. Dr. B. on a "bender", and kept me awake by pulling my blankets, and bothering me generally.—Marched at 3 A.M., and arrived at Bolton Station, 9 miles, on the Vicksburg and Jackson railroad, before the sun got hot. Bivouacked near the station. The boys have been getting green-corn out of "Jeff's" fields; and this evening I went blackberry hunting on his plantation—"Briar Field," I believe it is called: I know there were an abundance of *briars* and blackberries in some old fields that had been "turned out."[29]

July 3d.—Light shower. Some cannonading (the last guns fired) at Vicksburg. The guns were heard quite plain, as we are only 15 miles from the place.

July 4th.—All quiet to-day. Received orders to be ready to move at moment's notice.—

July 5th.—At 4 P.M., moved out and marched 6 miles towards Vicksburg, moving on the railroad, which is the hardest marching. The evening very hot. Division bivouacked in line of battle on the battle field of "Champion's Hill," or Baker's Creek. All are expecting hot work to-morrow. We are close to the Big Black, and have pontons ready to put down.

July 6th.—Fell in early and lo! instead of marching towards Vicksburg, the head of the column turned back towards Jackson. We are confident Johnston received the intelligence of the fall of Vicksburg last night. A hot and dusty march of 10 miles brought us to Clinton. We are bivouacked near town by a good spring. Heavy rain in the evening.

---

29. This was probably not "Brierfield," the Jefferson Davis plantation.

July 7th.—Marched by the Raymond road to Jackson, and bivouacked 2 miles below the city on Pearl river. This march of 15 miles has been about as disagreeable as we generally have. Water very scarce on the road. I had to straggle a little to-day.

July 8th.—The news had not been positively known to the troops of the fall of Vicksburg until to-day. The news cast a gloom over most of the troops, but did not seem to affect the "Orphans" much.

July 9th.—Before daylight news came in that the enemy was approaching, and ordered to be ready to move. At daylight marched to the suburbs of the city. Our division being on the left wing, the Ky. brigade rested on the river below the city and Adam's brigade extended on the right around to the Clinton road. As soon as our line was established, a party sent into the city to press negroes to work on the fortifications, and brought out quite a crowd to our regiment, among them a few dandy barbers, who did not fancy wielding the pick and shoving the spade much, but they had to go to work. After completing our works, we lay around loose, waiting the coming of events. Our line ran through a dutchman's garden, and we took his grape arbor for head quarters. I had to write part of the day, making out field return etc.

July 10th.—Early the enemy came in front, which was known by the pop, pop, popping of the sharpshooters. They did not come in front of our brigade, but in front of Adams on the right, and Stovall[30] in the center. Nothing further than sharpshooting, with a very little cannonading, on the lines to-day.

July 11th.—In the morning skirmishing all around the line save in front of our brigade. Not much cannonading from either side. Early in the forenoon Buford's Ky. brigade[31] had a pretty lively little fight on the extreme right of the army. At noon the brigade ordered across to the right to support Loring, an assault being expected on that part of the line. Our position was immediately in the rear of Col. Wither's fine mansion, the rifle pits running through his yard. The old Col., who was not in the service, had a musket on his shoulder ready to defend, or help defend, the works in front of his house. His mansion being exposed to artillery fire, he had moved all of his furniture out of the house into the back yard. A rain coming up soon after we got there, myself with others, volunteered to help him get his furniture

30. Marcellus A. Stovall.
31. Abraham Buford.

into the house again. He got all in at a back door save a large mahogany bedstead which we had to carry to the front door, where the Federal sharpshooters had full view of us, and gave us several rounds, but fortunately no one was hurt. I mention this, as it was the only adventure I had during the battle. Several of the brigade were wounded during the evening by sharpshooters. The enemy not assaulting, we returned to our old position late in the afternoon—The next day Col. Withers was killed, and when our army evacuated, his house was burned.

July 12th.—Early this morning Gen'l Hovey's[32] division charged in front of Stovall's and the right of our Brigade. He was repulsed with heavy loss, mostly inflicted by Cobb's battery of our brigade, and Slocum's[33] Washington Artillery of Adams' brigade. They came up square in front of these two batteries. We captured 3 stands of colors and about a hundred prisoners, that I saw. In the evening our regiment and the 2d moved to the rear of Cobb's and Slocum's batteries as a support; but late in the evening our regiment came back to old position, leaving the 2d.

July 13th.—Lying about all day idle, the enemy not being in our front. The city was subject to shelling at times during the day, and sharpshooting was kept up on both sides, with vigor.

July 14th.—Truce from 12 until 2 P.M. to allow the burying of the dead in front of our works. City shelled during the night.

July 15th.—Very quiet around the lines all day. Supposed that the enemy is waiting for arrival of ammunition train.

July 16th.—Heavy firing of small arms and cannon on the right about noon. Have not learned the cause. I can tell from the looks of affairs, we are going to retreat soon—no doubt to-night. As yet, there have been no Federals in front of us. They are in front of the 6th, on the right.

July 17th.—Last night, 16th, at 12 o'clock, fell in silently, and moved through the city, across the pontoon bridge over Pearl river, and marched out on the Brandon road. We were the last troops to cross the river; and the brigade moved in such good order, that it excited the admiration of the commanding Gen'l. It has covered so many retreats, the boys know just how such things have to be done. When daylight came, we were 4 miles from the city. Marched 14

---

32. Brigadier General Alvin P. Hovey, USA.
33. Captain C. H. Slocomb.

miles during the day, and bivouacked 2 miles east of Brandon. A very hot day, and dusty marching. All the troops having to move on the same road, we were delayed greatly.

July 18th.—Fooling along in rear of the wagon train all day. In the evening, the rain pourd down in torrents. After dark when we went into camp, or rather when we stopped for the night, every thing wet and disagreeable. I was too tired to go to the wagons for my blankets, and Col. W.[34] loaned me a blanket for the night. Have marched 16 miles to-day.

We remained at this place two or three days, having to cook rations nearly every day. We were on Dead River—and a *lifeless* looking place it is.

July 21st.—Marched 9 miles and bivouacked 4 miles east of Morton, a little town on the Southern R.R. Looking like rain we put up our fly and just as we drove the last pin, a heavy storm of rain came pelting down. The companies have neither flies nor tents, and the boys have to weather the storm as best they can. They generally, though, stretch their blankets up in the manner of a "dog-tent", which shelters them very well from the inclement weather.

Here we remained in camp, or bivouacked, a few days, the time passing monotonously. We had rain nearly every day. Water to drink was very scarce. The country perfectly level about camp and inclined to be swampy.

July 26th.—Orders to cook 4 days rations, preparatory, we think, to a march for Enterprise, Miss.

July 27th.—All quiet to-day—no prospect of a move soon. Every thing seems to be at a stand-still. Will probably move camp, however, very soon.

July 28th.—Moved camp 4 miles, and yet in 4 miles of Morton— Our march was through pine woods and broken country.

---

34. Lieutenant Colonel John C. Wickliffe had been promoted on April 22, 1863. Thompson, p. 449.

•5•

We Have Had Stirring Times: Chickamauga and Chattanooga

The Orphans spent a peaceful six weeks at Camp Hurricane. But then came another summons from their old nemesis Braxton Bragg, and off they went for Tennessee again. They reached the vicinity of Chickamauga Creek, in north Georgia, just in time for the Battle of Chickamauga, another of the high and low points of their war service. In the fierce fighting on September 20, 1863, they played a significant role in opening a hole in the enemy line, which led to the most complete defeat ever suffered by a major Union army. But in the same day's fighting, they lost yet another commander when General Helm took a mortal wound.

In the aftermath of Chickamauga, as the Confederates besieged the enemy at Chattanooga, Colonel Joseph Lewis of the 6th Kentucky took command of the brigade, and held it for the balance of the war. What could not be held, however, was the line of entrenchments Bragg had selected on Lookout Mountain and Missionary Ridge, facing Chattanooga. On November 23–25, the Federals, now commanded by Grant, broke out and drove Bragg back in a disgraceful rout. The Confederates had no choice but to retreat to Dalton, in north Georgia, where they would winter. If there was good news to be had at all, it was in the joining of the official 5th Kentucky Infantry to the brigade and, for all Kentuckians, in the welcome fact that Bragg was to be replaced as commander of the Army of Tennessee.

Now commences another long term of camp life, nothing going on to break the monotony, from one weeks end to another.

"Camp Hurricane," was situated among hills covered with pine. Our regiment camped on a hill nearly to itself, at the base of which was a large spring of excellent water, which supplied the division. The spring fed a mill-pond of considerable size, and under the mill, which was the smallest affair I ever saw, was a very excellent place for bathing. Our camp was on the margin of a small field, in the edge of which, stood a small cabin made of pine logs, the only evidence of civilization to be seen; all else around was an interminable forest of pines, the only growth these sterile hills can produce.

The boys built arbors of pine boughs which shielded them from the sun and in a great measure kept off the rain. We pitched the office in a pleasant place, and I was kept pretty busy at times writing. Lt. B.[1] left on a leave of absence and willed me his hammock while he remained away. I often tumbled out of it at night, while sleeping.

There was no field handy in which to drill, and the boys were glad of it.

A great deal of rain fell during our stay at "Hurricane", which mostly came of evening.

The spring was made a kind of market-place for the division, where soldiers would speculate in fruit, vegetables, etc. Large watermelons would sell for $40. The neighborhood of the spring was also being made a resort, for gambling, when Maj. "Hup" Graves[2] of Breckinridge's staff made a "descent" upon the sporting gentlemen, and broke up, such amusement.

I made the following notes: Aug 7th.—Got hold of "Great expectations," by Dickens. I partly read this book in Harper's Weekly, two years ago, while at sister M's. I shall now read it all under quite different circumstances. Aug. 11th.—Finished Great expectations today. Am well pleased with the book.—Aug. 21st. Being a day for fasting and prayer, had divine service near camp, under a large arbor built for the purpose.[3] Aug. 23d. Unwell—have been sick for several days—Aug. 24th. Heard from home through a friend.

---

1. First Lieutenant Joseph Benedict, Company B. Thompson, p. 815.

2. Major Rice E. Graves was chief of artillery on Breckinridge's staff. He was mortally wounded at Chickamauga, September 20, 1863. Thompson, pp. 458–59.

3. On August 21, 1863, Jackman was again formally detailed as adjutant's clerk. Jackman, Service Record.

Aug. 26th.—At 5 P.M. consigned our arbors to the flames, and marched towards Morton. Bivouacked near town for the night.

Aug. 27th.—All on the train by 10 A.M., and moved off for Meridian, where we arrived—the train ran very slowly—at 8 P.M. Immediately changed cars for Mobile. Train running all night.

Aug. 28th.—Just as the sun was coming up, could look down the long vista of pines, and see the tall chimneys of manufactories in the city, sending up their inky columns of smoke. Soon we were at the depot, and immediately moved to the steamer Natchez. Though we did not stay long in the city some of the boys had time enough to get on a "bender." Mobile looks about the same as it did a year ago, when we passed through—The steamer bore us out on the Bay and up the Tensaw, where we landed at the terminus of the Montgomery railroad. Disembarked, and bivouacked half a mile from the landings. The day pleasant and the scenery on the Bay beautiful. Right where we are camped there are no pine trees, which is quite a relief. The land here is a little hilly and looks to be productive.

Aug. 29th.—Took cars for Montgomery at 3.P.M.. Got to Pollard, touching a corner of Florida, at sun-down. Have been in the pines again for miles. Dark setting on, swung my hammock across the car, and went to sleep.

Aug. 30th.—Waked up at daylight and looking out the car, saw that we were still being whirled through pine forests. I judge from this, nothing but pines grow by the road its entire length. At sun-rise got into Montgomery, having been transported 162 miles by rail, since leaving Mobile. Immediately got off the cars and moved through the city, to the West Point depot and bivouacked in a pine grove on the common, waiting for transportation. Sunday, and the Church bells are ringing merrily—reminds me of peaceful days. In the evening went a muskadine [*sic*] hunting on the banks of the river, and got an abundance. To-night all the boys are in the city, having a general spree. Johnnie G.[4] and I, all that are left in camp.

Aug. 31st.—At 8 a.m., moved off on a train for West Point, where we arrived without incident at 4 P.M. At 7 changed cars and arrived at La Grange where we had to lay over from 10 until 1 o'clock. The depot at L. was thronged with ladies with nice provisions for us. I was asleep when the train stopped, and was waked up by a boy shov-

---

4. John W. Green, Company B, 9th Kentucky. Thompson, p. 819.

ing a broiled chicken into my face with other nice things to eat. I looked out at the platform in front of the depot where there was such a jam of white crinolines, and such a chattering of women, I thought at first I was in another world. We had a fine time, as the ladies stayed at the depot until midnight. We found refugees from Ky., and all parts of the South, among them.

Sept. 1st.—Arrived at Atlanta 9 a.m., and without changing cars, left for Chattanooga at 11 a.m. Got off the train 13 miles from Chattanooga 11 o'clock at night, and slept until morning on the side of the rail track.

Sept. 2d.—At noon got wagons to haul our baggage, moved 4 miles to Tyner Station, and went into camp. Tyner Station is on the Cleveland and Chattanooga rail road, about 12 miles, or less, from the latter place.

Remained in camp a few days nothing going on of interest. Had not been in camp but a day or so, when I was taken down with intermittent fever, but the Dr. took it in time, and broke it up.

Sept. 6th.—The division marched with two days cooked rations. Not having enough transportation to haul our baggage, I am left in camp until to-morrow, when wagons will be sent back for it. I am not well, but feel better.

Sept. 7th.—At noon to-day, Col. C. came back with orders to move the baggage of the division to Chicamauga station to be shipped to the rear. We had to be in a hurry too, for our army having left Chattanooga early this morning, there is danger of our being "gobbled." We had no wagons to move with, and had to "press" some in the country. Being appointed by the Col. to take charge of affairs, I sent two good fellows from our regiment out to "press" wagons, and had the other regiments to do likewise.

Soon our boys came back with an old ox-wagon which we kept busy hauling to the station, 2 miles, until dark. By that time all the "sick, lame, halt and blind," of the division were at the depot, and mountains of baggage. Had to telegraph for a train of cars to come up for us, which may not come until to-morrow evening or next day. This place is now unarmed, and in all probability, we'll be "gobbled" yet. When the last load was hauled, we honorably discharged "pompy" and his ox-team.

Sept. 8th.—Lying about the station all day. In the afternoon Bushrod Johnson's brigade came to the depot as a guard. We loaded on the cars late in the evening. On side-track all night.

Sept. 9th.—All the troops gone this morning. At sun-rise our train started down the road, but being so heavy, when we got to Graysville, 8-miles, the cars in which our brigade baggage is loaded left on the switch. Here Col. C. left me to "engineer" down the road as best I could. Late in the evening, the last engine was passing, and I got our cars on. We waited at Ringgold for the passenger train to leave, which was crowded with refugees. That night we ran down to Dalton.

Sept. 10th.—At Dalton all day. Very hot and dusty. Sick—have something like fever. There are so many cars here no telling when we shall get off—Dull—a man got his head shot off—in a row, during the evening, which was a little variety. Slept on top of a car at night.

Sept. 11th.—Left Dalton at 6 a.m., and arrived at Kingston, 40 miles, at noon. There we found Col. C., who had the baggage stored away in tents. Not being well, was left with it, with several others of regiment. Col. C. left for front, going by way of Rome. Kingston is a small woe-begone looking place, at the junction of the Rome road.

Sept. 12th.—Walked about 2 miles to have my clothes washed, but could not find any one to undertake the job. Am really sick. Dr. S. is giving me medicine.

Sept. 13th.—All quiet to-day. In the evening a train passed down with some of the 1st Ky. Federal Cavalry on board, that Forest[5] had captured at Tunnel Hill.

Got tired enough of Kingstown. We drew very good rations, and the "General," of our company, would go out "bear" hunting occasionally; and would also bring in sweet potatoes. I was sick all the while. Longstreet's Corps.[6] passed up the road during the time.

Sept. 17th.—To our great joy, Capt. N.[7] of our regiment, came down for all the officers' baggage, and all that were able to go to the regiment. This evening we came up to Resaca on the cars, and loaded the baggage on a wagon in waiting, and have footed it out 7 miles on the La Fayette road. We have a walk of 40 miles before us.

Sept. 18th.—About noon came to the road leading off to where the wagon train is encamped, we left the wagon, and started for the regiment. Part of the time our road led over steep hills, and had a very tiresome walk. In the evening, a party of us left the main road to

---

5. Major General Nathan Bedford Forrest.
6. Lieutenant General James Longstreet's I Corps, Army of Northern Virginia, had been sent by Robert E. Lee to reinforce Bragg's army in the Chickamauga campaign and arrived just in time to turn the tide in the battle of September 19–20.
7. Captain Price C. Newman, Company C, 9th Kentucky. Thompson, p. 825.

make a "near cut." There were 4 of us—Capt. N., 1st Seg't, J. F.[8] of his company, Dr. S., our Ass't Surg., and myself. We could hear the cannon booming occasionally. At night we stopped at a cabin on the roadside, and got a good supper. Then adjourned to a neighboring pine-thicket, where we passed the night, nearly freezing, as blankets were scarce.

Sept. 19th.—On the road early. Stopped at a well to wash and breakfast. A lady seeing us, sent out some butter and milk. Five miles brought us to the regiment near Glass' Mills. The brigade had just crossed Chicamauga River at Glass' Ford to support Cobbs' and Slocums' batteries, & the wickedest artillery duel ensued, I ever saw. Slocum and Cobb had to "limber to the rear" and move their batteries back across the river. There were several of our regiment wounded—three afterward, died of their wounds. About the middle of the afternoon moved a mile or two further to the right and halted in line of battle sending out skirmish line. While here we could hear the battle raging further to the right. But before sundown, our division again commenced moving to the right. At sundown, and a little after dark, the musketry rattled incessantly. I don't believe I ever heard heavier volleys of small arms. The word came back that Cleburn[9] was driving the enemy on the right. Having to move 5 or 6 miles, we continued our march until sometime after dark and the night being black, we had a deal of trouble. We at last crossed the Chicamauga at Alexander's Bridge, and not far from the bridge we stopped in an old field for the night. We built a large fire, yet not having any blankets with me, I did not sleep any. The night was very cold and my large overcoat came in good place.[10]

Sept. 20th.—Before daylight,[11] the division moved to take position in line of battle. After we had stopped for the night, the field band had been sent to the rear with the horses of the field and staff, and were not back in time; so the Col., etc., had to "foot it." The Col. left me at the fire to tell the musicians where to bring the horses. Daylight came and a heavy frost was on the ground. I waited until long after sunup, yet the drummers did not come; so I shouldered a long

---

8. James W. Ford, Company C, 9th Kentucky. Thompson, p. 828.
9. Major General Patrick R. Cleburne.
10. The entire Kentucky brigade had taken little part in the fighting of September 19, its involvement being limited to an artillery duel between Slocomb and Cobb's batteries and enemy cannon in the morning. Thompson, p. 216.
11. The division moved at 3 A.M. Thompson, p. 217.

bundle of blankets intended to be put on the horses, and started
for the regiment. I had to pass over the ground where Cleburn had
fought the evening before. The dead of both sides were lying thick
over the ground. I saw where six Federal soldiers had been killed
from behind one small tree, and where eight horses were lying dead,
harnessed to a Napoleon gun. Men and horses were lying so thick
over the field, one could hardly walk for them. I even saw a large
black dog lying mangled by a grape. In the rear of the brigade, I
found our ambulance, and put the blankets in it, then went on to the
regiment. The boys were lying in line of battle, and cracking jokes as
usual. Many of them I noticed to be in the finest spirits were in a
few minutes afterwards numbered with the slain. All the time the
skirmishers about two hundred yards on advance, were very noisy.
About 10 o'clock A.M. Maj. Wilson[12] rode up to Gen'l Helm, who
was sitting against a tree in "rear" of our regiment, talking to Col.
C., and gave him the verbal order from Breckinridge to advance in
fifteen minutes, and adjust his movements to the brigade on the
right. The General got up and mounted his horse, laughing and talking as though he was going on parade. I had intended to go along
with the infirmary corps, but as the drummers had not come up with
the horses, Col. C., ordered me to go back and see if I could find
them. I had not gone far, before I came to several of our boys that
had been wounded on the skirmish line and as the shells were tearing up the ground about them, which makes a helpless man feel very
uncomfortable, I helped put them in an ambulance and sent them to
a hospital. I went a little farther, in hopes of finding the drummers,
but they were nowhere to be found. I then started back for the regiment. The rattle of musketry was kept up pretty lively. As I passed
along over the field, could see all the little gullies were packed full
of straggling soldiers, (but I saw none of our Brigade among them)
avoiding the shells. When I got to the regiment it was just falling
back under a heavy fire, having charged three times unsuccessfully.
The regiment was greatly reduced—by half at least—Col. C. had
been wounded. Out of our company, my old friend J. H.[13] had fallen
with others and many had been wounded. Gen'l Helm had received
a mortal wound and had to be borne to the hospital on a litter. Lt.

---

12. Major James Wilson, formerly of Company B, 4th Kentucky, and afterward
Breckinridge's divisional adjutant general. Thompson, p. 630.
13. James Hunter, Company B, 9th Kentucky, was killed in the battle. Thompson,
p. 820.

Col. W.,[14] in command of the regiment, had me to ride the general's horse back to the hospital. Our brigade hospital was more than a mile from the field, across the Chicamauga. The wounded, I found, scattered over a half acre of ground—all out of our brigade too. Here I found one of the refugee drummers on Col. H's horse, which I immediately rode to the regiment, piloting Maj. Hope[15] and others to the brigade. The sun was then getting low and Col. W. immediately despatched me on his horse to the wagon train, or cook wagons, to hurry up the rations, the boys, not having had much to eat for two or three days. I had not been long gone, when our troops advanced again on the extreme right, and this time our brigade went over the enemy's works. The loss though, was nothing, compared to that of the morning fighting. When I got to the cook train, our wagon had gone to the regiment with rations, which I had accidentally passed in the darkness. I then rode back to the hospital, and stayed until morning.[16]

Sept. 21st.—As soon as it was light enough to see how to ride, I started for the regiment. I found them lying around loose, in line of battle, waiting orders. A skirmish line was soon after sent forward to find the enemy, but he had withdrawn during the night. The Army of Tennessee, *for once* had beaten the enemy in an open field fight. Gen'l Bragg rode along the lines, and everywhere was loudly cheered. We tried to get tools to bury our boys, but could not. Late in the evening, was sent with orders to the hospital, and remained there all night. After I had left, the brigade started towards Chattanooga. A detail was left to bury the dead.

Sept. 22d.—Early, Lieut. B. and myself followed up the regiment on horseback, and found it bivouacking on the side of the road, 4 or 5 miles from Chattanooga. Here we remained all night.

Sept. 23d.—In the forenoon marched over Missionary Ridge and formed line of battle around Chattanooga. We thought an assault was going to be made, and seeing the forts bristling with cannon, and the line of works blue with Federals, we had long faces. There were some shells thrown over us in the evening. At last "night drew her sable curtains 'round," and we lay down upon arms to sleep. Johnnie

---

14. Lieutenant Colonel John C. Wickliffe.

15. Major John S. Hope, Company G, 2d Kentucky Infantry. Thompson, p. 593.

16. On September 20, the Kentucky brigade saw very heavy involvement in the battle. Of approximately 1,300 engaged, 63 were killed and 408 wounded, amounting to more than 36 percent losses. Thompson, p. 219.

G. and I having pulled up a pile of dry grass upon which we lay, covered alone by our overcoats, and slept well.

Sept. 24th.—In the morning the division moved back to Missionary Ridge, immediately in front of Chattanooga, and formed our line a short distance above the base, and about 2 miles from town. Some shelling from the forts during the day, but generally quiet. About 11 o'clock at night our skirmish line advanced and drove the out posts into the works, creating quite a "fus[s]": but I don't believe a man was hurt on either side.

Sept. 25th.—Moved a little during the day, but at night occupied about the same position we did in the morning.

Sept. 26th.—Quiet all day. Making reports, and writing up my journal.

Sept. 27th.—Being Sunday, Prof. Pickett[17] preached for the brigade. He is brigade chaplain. Both armies seem to be taking a "blowing spell". No movements on either side, that I could see.

Sept. 28th.—Went to the wagon train—7 miles to the rear—and changed linnen after taking a bath in the "River of Death."[18] The ablution was quite necessary, for I had been in dirt for sometime past. At noon returned, and saw a train of 160 ambulances coming out of Chattanooga under flag of truce, for the Federal wounded that had been left on the field.

Oct. 1st.—Nothing of interest has taken place until to-day. A very *interesting*, cold autumnal rain has been pouring down all day and I have been crouched under a blanket, put up in the manner of a fly, all the dreary day. This has certainly been one of Bryant's "Melancholy days."[19]

Oct. 2d.—Rather warm. The brigade is out at the wagon train, and we are "cleaning up." Have been in the service two years to-day.

Oct. 3d.—In the evening moved back to our old position on the Bridge.

Oct. 4th.—All quiet around the lines. For several days past, a truce has been kept up between the pickets and we don't hear a gun.

---

17. Joseph D. Pickett, chaplain of the 2d Kentucky Infantry. Thompson, pp. 531, 817.

18. Lore in the army said the Chickamauga was an Indian word meaning "river of death." Davis, p. 192.

19. William Cullen Bryant, presumably.

In the evening moved our lines back up the hill a little, and commenced throwing up works. Our corn "doggers" and blue beef are sent to us daily, and in no great quantities.[20] We have our tent up, and pass the rainy days more comfortably than before.

Oct. 7th.—Raining in the forenoon. In the evening part of our lines subject to a few shells, thrown from the forts about Chattanooga.

Oct. 10th—All quiet until this morning, when we had reveille at 2, and the troops kept under arms, fearing an advance. To-day "Jeff" rode around the lines, and was generally loudly cheered. When he and Bragg, with other general officers, passed our lines, our boys stood very respectfully on the works, but not a man opened his mouth.[21]

Oct. 12th.—Wrote my first letter home, to send by flag of truce, *via* Richmond.[22]

Oct. 13th.—Raining since yesterday evening. Have lately seen several late Louisville Journals, gotten on the skirmish line. It seems despondent. Looks to be very wet and muddy, over in the "U.S."

Oct. 16th.—Cloudy and cool. "Novemberish." I have forgotten the date and it was of so little importance at the time, I did not make any note of it, but it was about this time, the fact was announced that Chattanooga was to be shelled from Lookout Mountain.[23] That morning, I clambered up to the top of the Ridge, to see the *grand sight*. The guns opened—little field pieces—and first we could see a little tuft of smoke rise out of the trees on the side of the mountain, then presently could hear the full report of the gun. Often the shells would fall short, and those that did go to the works, did no harm.

---

20. The corn "dodger" or "dogger" as Jackman spelled it, was a crude biscuit or cornbread made of coarsely ground cornmeal. "Blue beef" was a common nickname in both armies for the ill-preserved meat furnished to soldiers.

21. President Jefferson Davis visited Bragg's army after the Chickamauga victory, but the silence of the Kentuckians was not aimed at him. Their antipathy for Bragg had by this time become almost a religion. Davis, p. 194.

22. The only way for Kentuckians, whose homes lay behind Federal lines, to send letters home was by flag of truce, and channels for that purpose operated sporadically throughout the war. The uncertainty of the service is evidenced by how very few letters from Confederate Kentuckians have survived.

23. In fact, Longstreet's artillery did shell Chattanooga from Lookout Mountain, but it proved ineffectual.

Oct. 17th.—Day of sunshine. Great news from Virginia has been passing about to-day—something about Lee's whipping Meade.[24] It is also stated, in official circles, that Wheeler is on the rear of Rosecrans "playing smash."[25]

Oct. 20th.—Brigade moved back across the ridge, 2 or 3 miles, to the Chicamauga, and have gone regularly into camp. The October winds are filling the air with withered leaves, and soon the trees will be stripped. To be in camp again, makes one feel like he is at home.

Oct. 21st.—This morning had a light shower of rain, and a very heavy rain has just passed over this evening. A few such rains will entirely strip the trees. A good deal of fus[s] among the boys about the proper ownership of cooking utensils, which have not been used only by details of late. Often the "litigated" property is brought up to the Col's tent for a decision, and both parties invariably swear, or say they would be willing to "swear on a stack of bibles", as to the ownership of the doubtful property.

At 3 P.M., while a heavy rain was pelting down, received orders to strike tents and march. We crossed the Chicamauga on a pontoon bridge, and waded thru a swamp two or three miles wide, before we got to the solid road—when we marched for Tyner Station (which I have mentioned before), a distance of some 7 or 8 miles. The regiments got seperated in the swamp, and night overtaking us, we got lost. At last we came in sight of the camp-fires built by a detail sent foward in the evening for the purpose, and soon our troubles were forgotten in slumber.

Oct. 22d.—Sun rose in a cloudless sky and the day has been beautiful throughout. Commenced "fixing up" camp.

Oct. 23d.—Commenced raining this morning before daylight, and continued all day and greater part of the night also had heavy thunder.

Oct. 24th.—All last night the locomotives kept up a "tooting" over at the station. Longstreet's Corps shipped towards Knoxville.[26] To-day has been cold and cloudy—looks like snow.

---

24. This was undoubtedly news of the engagement at Bristoe Station, Virginia, October 14, 1863, the close of a six-day campaign that was not so much a defeat for Major General George G. Meade's Army of the Potomac as it was a punctuation of the status quo.

25. From September 30 to October 17, Major General Joseph Wheeler and his cavalry raided the communications lines of Rosecrans's army in Chattanooga.

26. Jackman is mistaken here, for Longstreet's command did not start to depart for Knoxville until November 4, though rumors of his orders to do so were circulating as early as November 1. It seems unlikely that Jackman would have heard of it on Octo-

Oct. 25th.—Sunday, and passed by without my knowing it being the Sabbath. A day of sunshine. Oct. 26th.—Another day of pleasant weather.

Oct. 27th.—Cloudy and sprinkling rain at times. Heavy firing of artillery at Chattanooga. Could not ascertain the cause.—28th.—Pretty day. Some cannonading at Chattanooga.—29th.—All quiet.

Oct. 30th.—Raining at reveille, and continued to pour down all day long. This weather is enough to give one the *ennui.*

Oct. 31st.—Stopped raining last night. Has been clear all day, but a cool disagreeable wind blowing. Regiment mustered for pay. Bro. Will staying all night with me.

Nov. 1st.—Sunday. Rode out 5 or 6 miles hunting black-haws and persimmons. Nice day.

Nov. 8th.—A cool north wind blowing. Being the Sabbath, Rev. Pickett preached this forenoon. Have been busy all the week, making out the different reports necessary to be made the first of each month. Had to work under difficulties. Rained all day Wednesday. Has been some cannonading at Chattanooga every day this week.

Nov. 9th.—Clear, cold. Last night ice formed ½ in thick first of season. 10th.—Froze ice again last night. Cobb's battery joined brig. from Miss'y ridge. Saturday the 5th Ky. joined the brig. in place of 41st ala., transferred.[27] Our brigade is now composed entirely of Kentuckians

Nov. 11th.—Johnnie G. and I commenced building us a house to-day, tearing down an old out house in the country for the purpose. All the boys are busy as beavers building cabins for winter. 12th.—Again, at work on house. Bro. Will was to see me to-day. He has been wrongfully placed in Water's[28] battery, which has been for

---

ber 24, however, for the movement had not yet been decided upon. Therefore, while the account of activity at the railroad depot on October 24 may be correct, almost certainly Jackman's explanation of it involving Longstreet is an after the fact addition. *O.R.*, series I, volume 31, part 1, p. 455.

27. Jackman here states that on Saturday, November 7, the official 5th Kentucky Infantry joined the brigade in place of the 41st Alabama. Its organization was now the 2d, 4th, 5th, 6th, and 9th Kentucky Infantries, and Cobb's battery. Davis, p. 195.

28. There was no Waters's battery with the army, though this certainly appears to be what Jackman is writing. He had previously written, then lined out, "Bate's battery," perhaps indicating that his brother William was assigned to a battery in the division commanded by Brigadier General William B. Bate. Jackman's later reference on December 2 that the battery's guns were abandoned on November 25 could indicate that his brother was with Cobb's Kentucky battery, all of whose guns were lost that day.

sometime stationed about Chattanooga. He was traveling on the cars with a pass from one of Wheeler's staff, which he thought was good: but he was arrested and assigned to the battery as a dismounted cavalry man. Col. W., to-day,* sent up a paper to Army Hd. Qrs., which will get him out of *"durance vile."*

Nov. 13th.—Rode over to the ridge to see Bro. W. When I got on the top of the ridge, I could but notice the change Autumn has wrought over the scenery. The trees are now all bare in the valley, and one can see all the movements of the troops, with more ease. There is a large army in Chattanooga. Grand scenery about, and I delayed for sometime beholding it, then went down at the base of the ridge and saw Bro. W., the battery being encamped on a little rocky elevation, out in the valley.

Nov. 14th.—Raining a little in the morning. 15th—Sun shining all day, but cold wind blowing. No Divine service—all the chaplains gone. 19th—Pretty day. Some cannonading at Chattanooga. Have just completed "our house." Weather has been beautiful the few days past. Yesterday wrote to J. L.,[29] 4 Ky. Cavalry. There has been more or less cannonading Sunday.

Nov. 21st.—Commenced raining last night and has kept up all day. Reading Burns by a good fire in "our house".

Nov. 22nd.—Bro. Will to see us. Has not got off yet. A clear and pleasant day.

I put the following letter in, as it gives an account of the movements of the brigade[†] during the Battle of Missionary Ridge, and retreat back to Dalton. The letter was printed in the Memphis Appeal, published at Atlanta, Ga.

My personal adventures were few. I saw a hard time.

The night we got to the Ridge, though late, thousands of camp fires were sparkling in the valley beneath. A belt of fires encircled Chattanooga, showing the lines of the enemy and all around the base of the Ridge, our fires were gleaming.

*[Jackman's marginal note is no longer extant.]
†The 6th Reg. was not with us at Missionary Ridge, having been left back at Chickamauga station to guard the stores &c.

29. Probably Jerry Leggett of the 4th Kentucky Cavalry. George D. Mosgrove, *Kentucky Cavaliers in Dixie* (Jackson, Tenn.: McCowatt-Mercer Press, 1957), p. 190.

Kentucky Brigade in the Late Battles.

We are permitted to publish the letter below, although a private one, from one friend to another, and not intended for the public eye. It will repay perusal, as it is well written, and evinces none of the fright and panic generally supposed to have existed throughout our army in the unfortunate battles at Missionary ridge:

Camp 9th Regiment Kentucky Volunteers,

Near Dalton, Ga., December 2d, 1863.

Dear _____ :[a]

We have had stirring times since you left; but taking all things into consideration, have come off pretty well. You have, no doubt, been kept posted as to the general movements of this army by the newspapers—I have not seen one since we left Tyner station—so I shall only attempt to give you a history of the part this regiment and brigade took in the late battle and retreat of the army.

The day after you left—Monday, November 23d—at 7 o'clock P.M., we broke up camp and marched for Missionary ridge, where we arrived at midnight, and stacked arms in line of battle, on top of the ridge, immediately above our old position. The following morning was cloudy and cold, and Gen. Lewis[b] moved the brigade into the ravine in rear of Gen. Breckinridge's headquarters, where there were some vacated winter quarters. We were not permitted to enjoy these long, for we were again moved to the top of the hill, about noon, and formed in line, single file, a little to the left of the position we occupied in the morning. The brigade immediately commenced throwing up breastworks, a little over the brow of the hill, toward Chattanooga. It commenced raining at 12 M, and continued until nearly night, being very disagreeable. The enemy could not have selected a more favorable day for storming Lookout mountain—the mist covered the greater part of it, and sometimes obscured the valley beneath from view. The batteries on Moccasin point, and at the Star fort, kept up a furious shelling nearly all day, their fire being directed at Lookout. The firing of small arms was incessant during the day, and long after night, when the flash of the guns seemed like myriads of fire flies on the mountain side.

The next morning, (25th) while the moon was in total eclipse, (about 2 A.M.) we moved to the right of Gen. Bragg's headquarters, two miles, (a little to the right of the tunnel, on the Chattanooga and Cleveland railroad,) and at daylight formed in line, as a reserve to General Smith's[c] brigade, Major-General Cleburne's division. We were attached to this division until we reached this place. Soon afterward, the 9th was moved to the front, and formed on the right of Gen. Smith, to fill up an interval between him and Liddell.[d] Here we had to "face the music" without pits or breastworks. However, as the enemy did not advance upon us but once, and then only in single line, we easily held our position. We were on the side of one hill, and the enemy had to charge down one opposite. They advanced about 9 or 10 o'clock A.M. We were under fire about twenty minutes when the Yankees fell back. A great deal of their fire was, I believe, directed at a Texas regiment on our left; that intended for us was mostly too high. There were only three men wounded in the regiment—Sergt. Young, Company D, through the left hip by minie ball, severely; Sergt. Carouth,

[a]The addressee of the letter is unknown.

[b]Brigadier General Joseph Lewis.

[c]James A. Smith.

[d]St. John R. Liddell.

color-bearer, a minie ball grazed his neck and breast, bruising him badly—he left the field only a few minutes; H. C. Johnson, company H, flesh wound through the left arm, by minie ball.[e] The enemy did not advance in our front any more. The 9th was the only regiment in the brigade that was engaged. The 2d came up and formed on our right afterward; but as the enemy did not again advance, they were not engaged during the day, the other regiments were held in reserve. All the fighting was to our left. In the afternoon the enemy charged—five lines deep—Gen. Smith, but were repulsed with heavy loss. His brigade was protected by heavy breastworks, hastily thrown up early on the morning. Awhile after dark we fell in and marched to Chick-amauga station. *I had no idea we were retreating until we reached the railroad bridge, when I saw them preparing to burn it.* I thought we were moving farther to the right for some purpose. The next day, (26th,) we had to cover the retreat, *as usual.* The brigade first took position in the works in front of Chickamauga station, then moved back on the range of hills in the rear of the station. While moving to the latter point, the Yankees shelled us—hurting no one. Soon two lines advanced on the right of the railroad, halted a little beyond the station, and sent forward two heavy lines of skir-mishers; as there was a probability of our being flanked on our right, we fell back, "by company to the rear," to the next range of hills, and formed "line-of-fight." This retro-grade was made at double-quick, but in order. The enemy did not press us further on this road, and we marched slowly towards Graysville. Before reaching that place, where another road came in, Generals Gist and Maney[f] were in line, expecting the enemy from that direction. We had not long passed them before they were engaged. At dark we crossed the bridge at Graysville, and as the road was clear, we made very good time to Ringgold, arriving there before midnight. While passing where a road intersected the one we were on, before reaching that place, leading to Chattanooga, the enemy, in ambush, fired into Ferguson's[g] battery, which was coming on immedi-ately in our rear. The brigade was formed in line quickly, at the base of a range of hills, which the road led over, then about faced and marched up the hill. The Yankees set up a most infernal howling, resembling a pack of wolves, which has succeeded in running down the prey. They were in strong force, and lucky for us, they did not reach the road in time to fire into our column. They forced Gist and Maney to come by another route. We stopped at Ringgold the balance of that night, and the next day the brigade was held in reserve to Gen. Cleburne. He succeeded in checking and driving back the enemy at Ringgold without our assistance. We camped at Tunnel Hill that night. The next morning the brigade was formed in line of battle this side of town, until Cleburne passed us, and then marched on the railroad to this place, arriving late in the evening.

Gen. Hardee is in command of the army now. Most of the field officers in this division went to town this evening to bid Gen. Bragg good-bye.

Cobb's battery was lost. His battery was not with us. It was on the ridge, some-where near Gen. Bragg's headquarters. He was supported by a brigade. Whenever he comes about this regiment the boys give him "fits" for trusting the battery in other hands.[h]

Yours truly,

J.

---

[e]Sergeant William Young, Company D, Sergeant David W. Caruth, Company B, and H. C. Johnson, Company H, 9th Kentucky Infantry. Thompson, pp. 837, 818, 852.
[f]States Rights Gist and George Maney.
[g]Captain T. B. Ferguson's South Carolina Battery.
[h]Cobb's battery was commanded by Lieutenant Frank Gracey while Cobb was tem-porarily absent.

When we stopped Johnnie G. and I made us a bed of brush, and tried to sleep, having no other covering than our overcoats—we left all our blankets in wagons—but the night was too cold: first a mist commenced falling, then soon after turned into snow or hail. We had to "nodd" around a fire all night. The next night a cold rain was pelting down, and while the boys were fortifying I tried to get a little sleep by lying down close to a fire. I did sleep a moment but burnt all the back out of my overcoat—or a big hole in it. Afterwards in the campaign, I often heard soldiers say, pointing me out, "Golly! didn't a *shell* come near getting that fellow: look at the hole in his coat."

The following morning, while going to the right, I saw Bro. W., who was still in the battery. I tried to get him to go with me, but he would not leave. I was standing immediately by Sg't Young, when he was shot, and I thought he was killed as the ball knocked him clear off the ground, and threw him several feet. When night came on, we all commenced piling up leaves, and building good fires, well satisfied that "all was well"; but we had scarcely laid down, before orders came for us to move. When we got back to Chicamauga station, the whole army was there in a "mess". I got a little sleep during the night, between Col. W. and Dr. B., who had blankets. The night we got to Ringgold, the boys had their choice to wade the stream, about waist deep, or go two miles farther, by a bridge, and many went around by the bridge, in preference to wading. Andy C.[30] and myself bargained with a teamster, who had a very small mule, to take us over, for which we were to pay him two dollars each. Andy is a very large man, and when we both got on the "mule" and pushed out into the river, he made demonstrations like he was going to his doom, and we had to use our heels with a vengeance to keep him from doing so. That morning, while we were in line near Chicamauga station, I was on the skirmish line with Company D. and all the troops fell back-unobserved by 4 or 5 of us, and we were surrounded before we knew it. We got out though by strategy, and fast running. I thought for a time, "Camp Chase" had one.[31]

I was worn out when we stopped at Tunnel Hill for the night. We had marched back and forth between Ringgold and Tunnel Hill, 7 miles, two or three times during the day, conforming our movements to Cleburn. After dark a rain set in and sleep was out of the ques-

---

30. Andrew Cronan, Company H, 9th Kentucky Infantry. Thompson, p. 850.

31. Jackman's reference is to the Union prison camp at Camp Chase, Ohio, where many Confederates taken in Tennessee and Georgia were imprisoned.

tion. When morning came, I did not feel very strong, and turned my Enfield, picked up on the Ridge, over to a gunless man. We had to stand in line-of-battle, in a pelting rain, until noon, when Cleburn passed us. Then we marched for Dalton on the railroad 6 or 7 miles. We stopped for the night in some old hospital buildings ½ mile from town, on the railroad. That night, Nov. 28th, I believe was the most disagreeable night I ever spent. The houses were not very tight, and I could not sleep on the floor inside, so I went out by a fire, and hovered around it all night long. I believe the keenest wind was blowing I ever felt. I had not slept any scarcely for 4 or 5 nights and could hardly hold my eyes open; yet I knew if I went to sleep, I would freeze.

Nov. 29th.—We moved a short distance up into a ravine to camp. Our wagons still being away, we had to "rough it" The night was again cold, and I got no sleep.

Nov. 30th.—To-day our wagons came up from Resaca. Johnnie G. and I immediately fixed up our fly—we had no tent—by weatherboarding the back end and building a large fire in front. At night, we had our blankets spread down on a bed of leaves, and slept "40 miles an hour."

Dec. 2d.—At night, received a letter from home by flag of truce, *via* City Point. Bro. W.'s battery was *fortunately* abandoned at the Ridge, and now he is with us.

•6•

We Have Seen More Fun To-day:
Winter Camp; Sherman Awaits

The winter of 1863–1864 in Dalton, Georgia, was a cold but peaceful one for the Orphans. John Jackman and the rest of them, like so many in the Confederacy that season, took part in the religious revival that swept through the army. There were also the usual entertainments, not the least of them the February 1864 election of delegates to the Confederate Congress in Richmond. Though Kentucky had never seceded, it was still represented, and since the only Kentuckians who could vote in a Confederate election were the men of the Orphan Brigade, a special campaign was conducted for them. The brigade was perhaps the only military unit of the war to elect its own public officials. Even more enjoyable for them was their leading role in the famous March 22 "snowball battle," which eventually involved thousands of frolicsome soldiers.

But there was sad news as well. Their beloved commander General Breckinridge was ordered away to the armies in Virginia, and could not take his Kentuckians with him. And lurking always in the backs of their minds was the knowledge that a massive Yankee army, commanded by William T. Sherman, was waiting for the warming of spring to begin a drive toward Atlanta.

Two or three days after, we moved camp over on the rail road, about a half-mile from town, and the boys immediately commenced putting up cabins for winter quarters. The nature of the ground does not permit the brigade to be all camped together and the different regiments have selected grounds to suit themselves. I like our "parish" finely. Bro. W., the day we moved, went to his command, Carter's scouts, which is encamped close to Dalton.[1]

Dec. 13th.—A rainy day. Being Sunday, the church bells are ringing in town, the first bells I have heard for sometime. For several days I have been too busy making reports to even write up my journal. To-day I have made a notebook out of old quartermaster blanks, and written up the days. (I have not copied all the notes, on account of putting the letter in, which is about the same in substance.)

Dec. 14th.—Johnnie G. and I have again commenced internal, or rather *external,* improvements. We built a chimney to our fly to-day.

Dec. 15th.—We have concluded to build a house for winter, and have been cutting and hauling pine logs for the purpose, to-day. The troops had four pounds of sweet potatoes issued to-day in lieu of bread. "Hard up." "Ike",[2] who has been over to the cavalry camp, says they are worse off. He says the "spurred" gentry are cutting down old trees, and robbing the wood-peckers of their winter stores of acorns, to the great discomfiture of the red-headed foresters. He says he saw an old wood-pecker expostulate in vain with a cavalryman, to leave her stores alone.

Dec. 16th.—All day, by request of Capt. B., A. I Gen'l of Brigade,[3] ruling out forms for blanks to be printed. Set in raining at dark—cold and disagreeable.

Dec. 17th.—Had quite a storm of wind and rain last night. Thanks to our "fly" for not leaking much. Looking over Murry's Encyclopaedia of Geography brought into camp by "Paul"[4] for the Col. to read. This old book came to me, like a friend of childhood's happy days, to call up pleasing reminiscences of times long ago. When a boy, many a

---

1. William Jackman served in Carter's Independent Battalion of Scouts, later Company G, 21st Tennessee Cavalry. Stanley Horn, ed., *Tennesseeans in the Civil War* (Nashville: Tennessee Civil War Centennial Commission, 1964), I, p. 101, II, p. 220.
2. Probably Isaac Bryant, Company B, 9th Kentucky Infantry. Thompson, p. 817.
3. Captain Samuel Buchanan. Thompson, p. 228.
4. "Paul" is obviously a nickname, and cannot be identified. Jackman later wrote this episode for publication in the *Southern Bivouac,* under the title "Foraging for Literature" (II, June 1884, pp. 457–58), again only identifying the protagonist as "Paul," an acting orderly.

winter evening was whiled away, combing over this book "Paul" made a bad selection for the Col., though, not being a book for the camp. Another time "Paul" was sent out to forage for literature, and came into camp with a Patent Office Report, and one of Cicero's works in Latin. "Paul" pretended to be one of the *literati*, but I doubt whether he was scarcely able to read. He handed the Col. the large book, the P.O. Report—and said he thought that a "pretty" good book; "but this one", he said, holding out the one in Latin, "is such d——d *bad print*, I don't know whether you can read it or not." It was excellent *print*, but "Paul" didn't understand the *nums, meums tuums*, etc. The Col. never sent him after books anymore.

Stopped raining at noon, and J.G. and I worked on our house, until Tattoo. 18th—Dec.—Clear.

Saturday, Dec. 19th.—Making Weekly Inspection Report—also made a blank for the brigade report, as a favor for Capt. B. Clear, but cool. 20th—In camp all day. No Divine service in camp. Clear, yet rather cool to be comfortable without. 21st.— Clear all day. At night wrote a letter for G.P.[5] to send home. He cannot write well with his left hand yet. (Lost his right hand at battle Hartsville.) My *fee* was a dozen oysters. *Paid!*

Dec. 22d.—In the forenoon, I "pulled off my coat and rolled up my sleeves" and *daubed* our new house. Quite a comfortable *mansion* for two to inhabit—it is also used for an office, as the roof is fly, which lets in plenty of light, so I can see how to write.[6] Afternoon visited Bro. W. and saw some horse racing, and came home. He came with me, and staid until 9 P.M.

---

5. George Pash, Company B, 9th Kentucky Infantry, had lost his right hand at the battle of Hartsville. Thompson, p. 822.

6. John W. Green, Company B, 9th Kentucky Infantry, Jackman's friend and housemate, left his own description of the erection of their hut, and Jackman's role in it. "John Jackman the Adjutants clerk, & I will build a hut for the Adjutants office & to serve as our own quarters," he wrote.

Jack is pretty good at such work if he was not so lazy. At home he was first a carpenter, then a school teacher & now a rather lazy soldier, but a christian gentleman. I have to keep at him though to get him to do any of the dirty & hard work.

We have however finally finished a very nice hut with pine poles, a tent fly for a roof & a stick chimney. The Jambs & the back of the fire place are built of rocks which are plentiful here. John is a good forager after reading matter & we have had from his efforts in that direction Jean Van Jean [*Les Miserables*], the Three Guards Men [*The Three Musketeers*] & the Bride of Lammermore. Kirwan, pp. 117–18.

Dec. 23d.—A cold disagreeable day. Had bean-soup, alone, for dinner, and for supper had "biled" rice, without sugar to sweeten it. To-night, have written another letter for G.P.

Dec. 24th.—Nothing going on of great interest. In the evening our Q.M. and Capt. G., owing to the proximity of "Christmas-times", and having taken on some "pine-top," were singing "The Star-Spangled Banner", with a *vim*.[7]

Dec. 25th.—A cold, cloudy, disagreeable day. Went to Church in Dalton, in forenoon and to-night. Have just written a letter home, to send by flag of truce. Set in raining late at night. My Christmas dinner was bean-soup without bread. The boys are not seeing a great deal of fun—some "tipsey".

Dec. 26th.—Cloudy, misting and raining. 27th.—Reading by a blazing fire all day, quite at home, the rain not ceasing to patter on our canvas roof. 28th.—Cool—cloudy at times. Made Inspection Rept. 29th.—Clear—pleasant. Dec. 30th.—a very pleasant day. Recording orders. Set in raining 9 P.M., and continued all night.

Dec. 31st.—Pouring down rain all day—the wind blowing and other disagreeable things. To-day one year ago, we were on "Wayne's Hill," Murfreesboro, listening to the music of shells.

Jan'y 1st. 1864.—The New-Year ushered in a very cold manner. Ground hard frozen this morning. The sun shone bright, yet a cool wind blowing in forenoon. Very cold to-night, out of doors. But the reckless winter winds that come sweeping over the bleak hills, roaring and snapping, screaming and shrieking, through the bare branches of the old oak, overhanging our abode, fail to penetrate the well chincked walls about us. There is a fire kindled on the earthen hearth, its convivial glow lending a perfect air of coziness to the little tenement.

Jany 2d.—Cold and clear—very cold.

Jany 3d.—Weather more moderate to-day. The regiment paid off to Oct. 31st, 1863. The commutation for clothing was also paid. I received about $33 commutation. Was kept busy all day, though Sunday, and did not attend Church. Bro. Will staying all night with me. Commenced raining after dark. 4th.—Rained some during the day. 5th—Too cold to rain. 6th—Disagreeably cold to-day.

---

7. John W. Gillum, Company A, 9th Kentucky Infantry. Thompson, p. 808. Regular mash or grain whiskey being in very short supply, Confederates often made their own out of fermented pine boughs, hence the nickname "pine top."

Jany 10th.—Wrote home by flag of truce, half page fools-cap. The U.S. stamp so torn, accidentally, I fear the letter will not go. Clear and cool to-day.

Jany 11th.—Cloudy, and sleeting at times. Bro. W. took dinner with us. Made Inspection Report afterwards.

Jany 12th.—Foggy this morning. Had hot biscuits, butter, molasses and stewed peaches for breakfast. Quite an improvement on our general bill of fair. Damp—appearance of snow.

The remainder of the week was pleasantest weather ever had; but the ground would freeze of night, and the next would thaw, making it very muddy about Camp.

Jany 17th.—Sunday. Went to Church in the forenoon and heard a good sermon.

There are three Protestant churches in Dalton—Baptist, Methodist and Presbyterian. There is also a very neat Catholic church in town. Of Sundays, these churches are generally full to overflowing, with soldiers. Chaplains from the Army generally officiate. Many soldiers go to church just to get sight of a lady

Jany 18th.—The following letter written on this date will give a little insight as to the way we are living.

Letter from the Army.
    In Camp near Dalton, Jan. 18, 1864.

Editors Appeal: The rain, how it patters down this morning, how gloomy without. We were gladdened yesterday by the sunlight, which fell in a golden flood on the surrounding hills, on the slopes of which are the rude villages—the present abiding place of our army. The inhabitants were enticed out of their cabins, in which they had been confined for some time by the frosty weather, and they perched upon the piles of wood in the streets, to sun themselves, chattering away merrily, happy that the crystal bars of winter were broken for a time. But the rain is come, and with it slush and mud, making it more disgreeable than ever in camp. For some time past, owing to the inclemency of the weather, all drills, reviews, etc., have been omitted, but will, no doubt, be doubled as soon as the mud becomes "navigable," in order that this army may be in the best possible trim to give United States Grant a warm reception when he is met in the coming spring.

Our habitations are pleasantly situated on the hills, and add a strange beauty to the surrounding scenery, which is naturally romantic, while the blue columns of smoke, curling up from the rude chimneys, speak of comfort to the weather-beaten soldier. It is amusing to go through the camps, to see the many plans after which the "dwellings" are built; they are of as many different shapes as has Proteus, while all manner of rough architecture is displayed. Yet, in every case, the well chincked walls shield the inmates from the rude blasts of winter, and are generally comfortable, no matter what the over-fastidious may say to the contrary.

In passing through these soldier towns, one may observe that the spirit of speculation has crept into the army to some extent. The trade is principally confined to "gingerbread" and "goobers," which are temptingly displayed at many cabin doors for sale. There are also restaurants in full blast, where a cup of "genuwine" Misc. with "etceteries," can be had at all hours. On the railroad, which is the thoroughfare between camps and town, a drinking saloon is sometimes opened, in the shape of a man, with several canteens swung around his neck, who doles out the "pine top" at the moderate rate of two dollars a drink. There is generally a crowd around this "saloon," which seems to do a thriving business in a small way.

Camp life is not so horrible as one might suppose. The "old heroes of an hundred battles" assemble around the roaring log fires, kindled on their earthen hearths, some to talk of the gay times they will have "when this cruel war is over," to recount their adventures and hardships in former campaigns, and to speculate on those to be made in the future; and, not seldom, to talk of their faraway homes, many of which are in the lines of the enemy; others again read their bibles by the light of a blazing pine-knot—"soldier's candles"—while many seek amusement in the mysteries of "seven-up," "poker," and other games. Thus are the long winter evenings whiled away. When wearied, they retire to their rough couches, perhaps to wander in sweet dreams to their faraway homes, and are surrounded by loved ones. Ah! many can visit their homes only in dreams. They have been driven back, step by step, dying their native soil with their blood—driven into exile. What a proud day it will be to these exiled-veterans, when the foe is hurled back from our borders, and they can once again cross their threshholds in reality, to meet the dear ones from whom they have been separated so long.

The winter is wearing away, and soon our battle flags will have to be unfurled to the breezes of spring, and the lines of gray will have to be drawn up—a living wall, against which the tide of invasion, it is hoped, will beat in vain.

The old year closed down upon us with defeat, disaster. May the present year bring us victory and success. The hour is dark and full of gloom, but such generally comes before the dawning of beautiful day.

When the above was written, the rain was pelting down. This morning, 19th, there is a great change in the weather. We had a light fall of snow last night, costuming the hills in white robes. Early the sun struggled through huge piles of dark clouds, which were soon dispersed, leaving a clear sky and bright sun; and already the snow has nearly disappeared, except on the mountains which "loom up," dazzling white, in the distance, presenting very beautiful scenery.

Stopped raining at noon and turned cold—will probably snow.

This morning, Prof. Pickett spoke to the regiment, recommending that they vote for Congressmen, to represent us in the Confederate Congress. We are at issue in reference to this matter. As Kentucky has never seceded, electing Congressmen to represent the state in the Confederate Congress, is all a humbug.[8]

Jany 19th.—A light fall of snow last night, which soon melted away, save on the distant hills, where it lies glittering white in the light of the winter sun. 20th.—Beautiful day.

Jany 21st.—Gen'ls Johnston and Hardee inspected the troops and camp of the brigade to-day. At night went to church in town. Some Chaplain from the Army preached from *"Wisdom is better than weapons of war."* From the way things look about here, there is but little *wisdom* in this locality.

Noisy over on the left of the reg't at night. Must be having an "Irish Wake."

Jany 24th.—Being the Sabbath attended Divine Service at the Baptist Church. Had a most able sermon from the Rev. Doctor Joseph C. Stiles, of Savannah, Georgia, a Presbyterian, I believe. His sermon smacked greatly of politics. I believe he is one of the ablest Divines I ever heard speak. At night, had a sermon at the same place, from Dr. Flyor, an army Chaplain.

Jany 25th.—In forenoon the brigade was "bugled" out into an old field near our camp. The attendance was not compulsory—and some of the aspirants for Congress spoke to the boys. The old politicians, I see, have not forgotten how to "work the wires." The following candidates spoke: Dr. Johnson,[9] about the size of Humphry Marshall and a surgeon in the army; Maj. Geo. W. Triplett[10], our old brigade quartermaster; Judge Moor,[11] who is at present a member from the upper part of the state; Col. M. H. Cofer,[12] of the 6th Ky; Seg't Maj. Marshall[13] of the 4th Ky and Col. Phil Thomson[14] a member of the provisional government of Ky. The following, though not candidates

---

8. Since Kentucky itself was behind Union lines, no elections could be held there to send representatives to the Confederate Congress in Richmond. As a result, the election was held among the only Confederate Kentuckians able to vote, the First Kentucky Brigade, making them probably the only military unit in American history to have their own congressmen. Davis, pp. 207–8.

9. Thomas Johnson. Thompson, p. 40.

10. Major George W. Triplett, 1st Kentucky Cavalry. Thompson, pp. 150, 995.

11. James W. Moore. Davis, p. 207.

12. Colonel Martin H. Cofer, 6th Kentucky Infantry. Thompson, p. 425.

13. Sergeant Major John L. Marshall, Company I, 4th Kentucky Infantry. Thompson, p. 680.

14. Philip B. Thompson, who later commanded Breckinridge's bodyguard. Thompson, p. 40.

spoke: Col. Phil Lee[15] of the 2d Ky., and Capt. Stanley,[16] of the 6th Ky. The "state" of Kentucky, being present, *en masse*, the speakers "spread themselves," and "the state" cheered. M. Langhorn[17] of our "mess", is a candidate, but he was not present to speak.

Feby 5th.—Grand review of the army by Gen'l Johnston to-day. A beautiful day for the occasion. This review took place in a large field south of town, half a mile. The troops were formed in three parallel lines, each nearly, or quite two miles in length. After the Gen'l rode up and down the lines, going in front and rear of each, he took his station at a point for all to pass on review. At this point, a great number of ladies, citizens and loafing soldiers, were assembled, myself being among the latter. I heard the Gen'l tell his wife there were 40 thousand troops, in line, on the field, and thinking it a "story", I thought I would make an estimate. There were 87 regiments and battalions present and I put down the infantry as between 23 and 25,000. I made no estimate of the artillery. There was one brigade on outpost, and Cleburne's division was away. The cavalry was not present. The troops as a general thing, did not march well. Our brigade did finely, and so another brigade or two. Some commands came "ganging" by, like flocks of sheep.

Feby. 7th.—Attended divine service in town this morning. At 2 P.M. attended a meeting at the Presbyterian Church for the purpose of forming a Christian Association for Lewis' brigade, but did not participate in the proceeding.

Feby. 11th.—At night the brigade went into town to see Gen'l Breckinridge, and pay respects, he being on the eve of leaving for the Department of Western Virginia. He made the boys a little speech, stating he was making every effort to have the brigade transferred to his new department. He then made a few happy remarks about Kentucky, etc. The boys are anxious to go with him, so as to be nearer home. The Gen'l seldom speaks in public, then only to our brigade.[18]

---

15. Lieutenant Colonel Philip Lightfoot Lee, 2d Kentucky Infantry. Thompson, pp. 400–401.

16. Captain William Stanley, Company G, 6th Kentucky Infantry. Thompson, p. 785.

17. Sergeant Maurice Langhorne, Graves's battery. Thompson, p. 860.

18. In his speech, Breckinridge told the Kentuckians that they were themselves the cause of their not being allowed to accompany him to Virginia, "as their good marching, great endurance, and gallant fighting had given them a position there that would be hard for any other brigade to fill." Thompson, p. 234.

Feby 22d.—Just before Tattoo, I noticed horses hoofs clattering over the road towards Army HdQrs. A courier of course from the front and I remarked that something had "turned up". Sure enough, orders soon came in to be ready to move at a moments notice, and to be prepared for action and to cook two days rations I went to bed at 12 o'clock, but had scarcely given up to "natures sweet restorer", when an "orderly-call" was rattled on the drum, and orders given to be ready to move at daylight.

Feby 23d.—We have again taken the "Warpath"—have left our snug winter quarters, and are now only sheltered by the broad canopy of the heavens. At day light all our baggage was loaded and the trains started for the rear. Every thing has the appearance of a retreat. At 3 P.M., our brigade moved up to Mill Spring or Creek Gap, 2 miles west of Dalton, and formed lines on a ridge, at the east end of the Gap. This Gap is made through Rocky-face Ridge by the flow of Mill Creek, a considerable stream, and it is through this Gap, the rail road passes leading from Chattanooga to Atlanta. Seeing the troops clambering up the steep hills, on either side of the Gap reminded me of pictures seen of Hannibal crossing the Alps. We are held in reserve. The day has been beautiful—springlike. Shall have to sleep on the ground, and no doubt sadly miss the cozy shantee in which we have been passing the winter.

Feby 24th.—This morning is one of sun-shine. We are quietly resting on arms—not having heard a hostile gun yet. The news from the front is, that the enemy is advancing in strong force, slowly, and are about Tunnell Hill, the main body having camped at Ringgold last night. Our troops are still coming up from the rear, and are in fine spirits. Things don't look so much like a retreat now—more like "fight."

9 P.M. I write by the light of a camp fire. All was quiet to-day, save now-and-then the thunder of cannon would come from the front, until about 4 o'clock in the evening. Then the skirmishers in front commenced a lively popping, our cavalry coming back to the rear, and one of our batteries opened in the gap. The enemy has not fired any "shrieking" shells yet—that is, none have come over us: we are some distance in rear of the front line. Just before sun down the brigade moved to the right across the railroad as a support to Steward,[19] who was having quite a lively skirmish. A little after dark we moved back

---

19. Major General Alexander P. Stewart.

to our old position. Clayton's[20] brigade on the right, had quite a battle this evening before sundown, the fighting taking place in his old camp. He drove the enemy back. The boys are now sleeping on their arms,—taking a good night's rest, believing the morrow will bring the storm of battle.

Feb. 25th.—I write at 8 P.M. Contrary to expectation, we have not been engaged to-day. We moved very little. Late in the evening we clambered about half way up "Buzzard Roost," to our left, but at twilight came back to our old "stamping-ground." In the forenoon, all quiet around the lines, but as evening advanced, considerable cannonading in the Gap, and farther to the right. We had a few of the "shriekers" to pass over us in the afternoon. Saw a pretty lively skirmish to the right of the railroad this evening. Clayton again drove the enemy back on the right—heavy fighting reported up there. A good deal of "sensational" from the right, in fact. All is quiet now, though awhile after dark, an occasional cannon was heard, and the sharpshooters would stir-up a fuss. Thousands of camp-fires are blazing on the hills, and in the valleys. To-morrow, undoubtedly, the "ball" will open in earnest.

Feby 26th.—I write at half past 9 a.m. Save an occasional report of a sharpshooter's gun, all is now quiet. Just as day was dawning, the skirmishers commenced firing pretty briskly, which caused the boys to spring to arms—a good reveille. Cool wind blowing from north east. Sun shining brightly. Rumor says the enemy took Dug Gap, 4 miles to our left, yesterday evening. I had a good night's rest on a "pallet" of boards.

9 P.M.—Nothing of interest has taken place to-day—there has not even been any cannonading. The skirmishers, also, have kept moderately quiet. Has been a beautiful day. Now the stars are twinkling in cloudless heavens. Nothing is heard, save a squeaking violin, which some soldier of a musical turn has brought out on the field with him, and the occasional hooting of an owl, from the neighboring forest. The hills and valleys are lit up by thousands of bivouac's fires. We moved none to-day. Our position is on a spur of the main hill, which spur juts out into the valley, at the east entrance of the Gap. At its terminus on the creek, the side is very steep, and on the side next the enemy. A few trees stand on top of the ridge—the east slope being a cornfield.

---

20. Brigadier General Henry D. Clayton.

Feby 27th.—At 10 a.m. our skirmishers advanced and found the enemy had gone back during the night. I have learned the Federal army had all passed through Tunnel Hill by 10 P.M.

I have been fooled twice in this movement. First I thought we were going to retreat back towards Atlanta—then later I thought we were going to have a big battle. We neither retreated, nor had to fight much.—Pretty day.

Feby 28th.—At 10 a.m. marched back to our old camp, which we found *in status quo*, and the wagons back. It did not require us long to go to "house keeping" again.

Feby 29th.—Commenced raining last night, and continued through the day, until late in the evening, when the weather turned cold—wintery. Lucky for us we are in camp. Received a letter from home, dated Feby 3d, sent by flag of truce. Read it over a dozen times. The second letter, received by "F.T."

March 2d.—Clear and cold. Wrote a letter home—also wrote one for George P——.

March 6th.—Sunday. Attended church in Dalton, and heard a very good sermon by the Rev. Dr. McFerrin,[21] formerly editor of the Methodist Christian Advocate, Nashville. Went again at night: Rev. Weaver[22] of Ga. spoke. Eight or ten soldiers joined the church. Nothing of interest in the military line this week. Latter part of the week, weather clear—nights cool.

March 7th.—Considerable hail and rain, with thunder.

March 8th.—Received a letter from home by flag of truce, dated Feby. 10th, and answered it immediately. Went to church at night and heard Dr. McFerrin speak.

March 9th.—Did not send my letter home until to-day. Went to church again to-night and heard Dr. McF. The church (Baptist) is crowded full of soldiers every night. Many are joining. Set in raining & I had to come home through it.

March 10th.—Bright and clear this morning—beautiful morning. Received a letter from my old friend J.W.L.[23] of 4th Ky. Cavalry. Bro. W. called to see me at noon, and remained several hours. His command will start to-morrow for the rear to recruit.

21. The Rev. John B. McFerrin. "Relics at the Centennial Exposition," *Confederate Veteran*, V (November 1897), p. 562.

22. Charles C. Weaver. "The Last Roll," *Confederate Veteran* XXI (March 1913), p. 135.

23. Probably Jerry Leggett, 4th Kentucky Cavalry. Mosgrove, p. 190.

March 13th.—Sunday. A beautiful day. Went to church in forenoon
and heard a good sermon by Rev. Payne. At church again at night.
Attended church several nights during the week—no place else to go.

March 14th.—Wrote to J.W.L. Fine weather. Looking for a letter
from home.

March 20th.—Went to the Baptish church in forenoon to hear
Brig. Gen'l Pendleton, Chief of Artillery in Lee's army, preach.[24]
He is Episcopal. An old man, gray beard, and stoutly built. Gen'ls
Johnston and Hardee were present, with many other generals. House
very much crowded. At 2 P.M. Rev. Roberts, a Baptist Missionary
to the army, preached near our camp. Went to Bap. chch at night.—
All quiet in military circles, the past week. Of nights, the soldiers
are generally at church in town. I went several nights during the
week.

Tuesday, March 22d.—Last night the snow fell three or four inches
deep, and continued snowing, not very hard though, through the
day. We have seen more fun to-day than at any one time during the
war. Early in the morning, the 4th Ky., whose camp is near Tyler's[25]
brigade of our division, got up a snow fight with Tyler's men, and all
the other regiments in our brigade went to reinforce the 4th. After
fighting awhile, our brigade and Tyler's "made friends" and both
went over to Finley's[26] Fla. brigade of our division, and charged the
camp. Finley was soon "cleaned out." Not having seen enough fun,
our division (Bate's[27]) marched on Stovall's brigade,[28] Stewart's[29] division, two miles off. We marched in military order, and when we
got in the neighborhood of the camp, sent forward, after forming
lines of battle, a line of skirmishers to develop the enemy. Our skirmishers soon had to fall back before superior numbers, and we made
a general assault. We took the camp with so little fighting—not having seen near sport enough—our lines fell back, and let Stovall's men
prepare for defense. By this time, Gen'l S.[30] came in person, and
had his brigade formed. We charged again, and took a stand of col-

24. Brigadier General William N. Pendleton.
25. Brigadier General Robert C. Tyler took command briefly of Bate's brigade,
when Bate replaced Breckinridge at the head of the division.
26. Brigadier General Jesse J. Finley.
27. Major General William B. Bate.
28. Brigadier General Marcellus A. Stovall.
29. Alexander P. Stewart.
30. Marcellus A. Stovall.

ors, and Gen'l S. himself. Lt. McC.,[31] and myself had the honor to capture the flag, which we brought to camp. Having entirely demoralized Stovall, we came home. I got several bruises.

In the afternoon, a courier came over from Tyler's brigade, stating that all of Stewart's division was advancing on our division. Soon our regiments were marching to the half-way grounds, which was to be the seat of war. We formed our lines in a range of hills, and waited for the enemy, after sending out skirmishers. Had not been in line long, when we could see the red banners of the advancing hosts, contrasting beautifully with the white snow. They came steadily forward, and soon the air was full of snow-balls. Before the action commenced, our Q.M.,[32] who had the honor to comd. our regiment—and we had the honor to be commanded by him—made us a stirring speech. All of Stewart's men had ten rounds each of snow-balls in their haversacks, and we had to fall back. I recd. a wound in the left eye, in the early part of the action. Q.M. came near being captured, only saving himself by putting spurs to his horse. As we were driven through Finley's and Tyler's camps, their men deserted us, and we still had to retreat before superior numbers. We took advantage of ground occasionally, and gave the overpowering columns a check. A detachment of our men captured Gen'l Stewart. At last when they had driven us back to the camp of the 4th Ky., our regiment made a flank movement, which so surprised the enemy, he was soon put to rout, and our camp saved from pillage. The 4th & 2d, lost their flags. We took out the banner captured from the 47th Ga., Stovall's brigade—I believe it was the 47th—perhaps the 41st—and we brought it back with us.[33] Lt. McC. acted as color sergeant, and I as his guard. After we had routed the enemy, we captured many prisoners, among them Maj. Austin,[34] of La., who occasionally gives us something to laugh at, over the name of "Maj. Cherrycomb."—To-night I feel "terribly" sore.

March 23d.—The sun shining this morning, and the snow is rapidly disappearing. Feel so sore from my sport yesterday, I can scarcely move. The boys want me to write an account of the late battle and have it published, but I feel too crippled.

---

31. First Lieutenant Thomas A. McLean, Company A, 9th Kentucky Infantry. Thompson, p. 808.
32. Captain J. Mort Parry, Company A, 9th Kentucky Infantry. Thompson, p. 808.
33. It was the flag of the 41st Georgia. *O.R.*, series I, volume 32, part 2, p. 589.
34. Major J. F. Austin, 14th Battalion Louisiana Sharpshooters.

March 25th.—Wind blew very hard last night, bringing up a snow storm. The ground was white again this morning with snow, but it soon melted away. The brigade has gone out to the execution of the sentence of a court martial on one Keen, of the 2d Fla. reg't, who is to be shot for desertion. This is a murky day—I would hate to be shot on such a day—especially for desertion.

March 27th.—Sunday. Had a cup of genuine coffee this morning for breakfast—something unusual. A beautiful morning—very spring-like. Went to church 10 a.m. in Dalton. Heard a good discourse by Rev. Taylor. I attended church again at night, heard a good discourse by the Rev. Hutchins, of Mobile, Ala.—To-day has been beautiful throughout. I think the winter is now over. The spring-birds have set up their songs in the thickets; and this morning I heard the cooing of a dove—the first of the season.

March 28th.—Cloudy, and cold wind from the east. Rain dashes down at times. Wrote a letter home for G.P. Steady rain in the evening until nearly dark, when the clouds broke away, and the cold east wind again set in. Late at night had a storm of wind and rain.

March 29th.—A spring-like morning. This is truly changable weather. Had no rations to cook for breakfast. Has been a peculiar day. As it advanced, a mist settled over the hills, veiling the sun from view.

March 30th.—A cloudy cheerless day. A few snow-flakes whirling in the air this morning.

March 31st.—Went to the old field south of town to witness sham battle between Cleburne's and Bates' divisions, against Cheatham's[35] and Walkers[36]—all of Hardee's corps. The day was pretty and the troops manoeuvered well; but there was nothing very exciting about the drill. Had stewed peaches and corn bread for dinner. Went to church at night & heard Dr. McFerrin. Rained during the night.

April 1st.—Had corn bread "straight" for breakfast—baked beef and Irish potatoes for dinner. Cloudy and sometimes rainy during the day. Being the first of the month, had to make several reports. O. what a gloomy evening! Capt. W.[37] showed me a book this evening, which, if I ever become again civilized, I shall obtain a copy: The elementary French reader; or Easy Method for Beginers in translat-

---

35. Major General Benjamin F. Cheatham.
36. Major General William H. T. Walker.
37. Probably Captain John J. Williams, Company G, 9th Kentucky Infantry. Thompson, p. 838.

ing French, etc., by Norman Pinney, A.M. Capt. W. has been looking over it a week or so, and can already read French pretty well.

Saturday, April 2d.—A murky day. Made Monthly Return. Nothing going on of interest.

April 3d.—Sunday. A pleasant morning, nearly clear—a few white tufts of cloud, floating about in the heavens. Went to church at 10 a.m. Heard Reverend Hutchins; and again at night, Dr. McFerrin speaking.

April 4th.—Raining this morning—the cold east wind dashing the rain against our canvas roof—very disagreeable. Raining at times during the whole day; but just before the sun retired, he smiled upon us, through the inky masses of cloud, which had broken into fragments. Nearly always see Gen'l B. F. Cheatham at church.

April 5th.—Cloudy, not cold, but disagreeable. At church to-night. A very young man preached—he will do better, I hope, when he grows older. I believe there has been church in town every night since the army has been here.

April 6th.—The sun has been shining all day—very pleasant—spring-like. I hope the the winter is now over.—Some cannonading in front. Probably our neighbors at Chattanooga are also having sham battles.

April 7th.—Our corps had another sham battle to-day, Cleburne and Bate, against Cheatham & Walker, this time using blank cartridges. Many people were on the ground to witness the scene. Ladies from nearly every city in the south, or in Georgia, rather, were present. The spectators were on a hill hard-by, where they could see all the manoeuvering. The firing sounded very much like a battle. The cavalry charged our division, and we were formed in oblique squares. Our boys shot wads at the spurred gentlemen, and wounded one or two pretty badly. In the morning the rain commenced, but soon stopped, and we had a beautiful day for the occasion. Clouded up again in the evening.

April 8th.—Raining this morning. Being a day for fasting, etc., went to the Baptist church at 10 a.m., and heard a young preacher. At 3 P.M. Had a discourse from Rev. Dr. Teezdell, or Tesdel, a Baptist minister from Mississippi. He is a venerable looking man, and a man of great intelligence. Had showers during the day, and after dark, the rain poured down in torrents for a few hours.

April 9th.—The sun is coming up clear and bright, and the birds are singing merrily—happy, it seems, the rain is over. Clouded up in the evening. Went to church, and had to come home through the rain. A cold north wind blowing.

April 10th.—Sunday—cloudy, wind from the east. Every sunday morning, have general inspection of arms, quarters etc., at 8 o'clock. Went to church in town. Dr. Teesdell spoke. At night went back again and heard Brig. Gen'l Lowery[38] of our army, a Baptist. He is a close reasoner, and spoke eloquently. He seemed in earnest, not merely speaking that the boys might hear a *General*. He is a tall military looking man, about 30 years of age, from appearance. I am not sure but I believe he is from Alabama.

April 11th.—Beautiful this morning. The birds seem rejoicing, as well as man, at the return of pleasant weather, for they are singing merrily enough. Heard Rev. Worrel, an editor. He edits the "Soldiers Friend," published at Atlanta. I don't think him of much force. Wrote home.

April 12th.—Raining this morning at daylight; but cleared up again—showers during the day. Went to church at night through the rain; but when I came back, the moon shining brightly. Dr. Teesdell spoke.

April 13th.—Beautiful day throughout. The flowers are blooming, and the trees leaving out. I welcome the spring-time. At night went to church. Rev. Roberts spoke. He is an "old chap," full of zeal— lives at La Grange, Ga.

April 14th.—Cloudy this morning—looks like rain.—At night went to the Methodist church. The different denominations have been meeting at the Baptist church until now. They have gotten up a row, and have divided off. I did not learn the man's name who preached.

April 15th.—Rained a little in the morning, but turned out to be a delightful day.

April 16th.—Pretty morning. Have not had any newspapers for a week, owing to the strike of the printers at Atlanta. I feel at a loss without the daily papers—don't know what is going on in the world. Looking for flag-of-truce letters, as two days have passed since a boat arrived at City Point. This evening an army Missionary preached near our camp. Prof. Pickett was present.[39] He is in bad health and has not been with the brigade a great deal this winter. He stays at

---

38. Brigadier General Mark P. Lowery was, in fact, a native of Tennessee, aged 35. Warner, p. 195.

39. Joseph Desha Pickett. Thompson, p. 532.

Atlanta. At night went to the Baptist church in town and heard Rev. O'Kelley, the first Irish protestant I ever heard. He spoke well.

April 17th.—Sunday. In the morning attended Baptist church and heard O'Kelley. Rev. Roberts baptized 17 soldiers near Bates' old brigade in the afternoon. Slight fall of rain set in at dark.

April 18th.—Clear to-day, save at noon had an April shower and some thunder. Cool wind from the north to-night. Heard Gen'l Lowery preach at night.

April 19th.—Cloud and sunshine. Cool wind from the north. Gen'l Johnston reviewed the army to-day on the usual grounds. The troops did pretty well—seem in good spirits.

April 20th.—Clear and more pleasant to-day. Our neighbors at Chattanooga must be having another sham battle, as I hear heavy firing of artillery in that direction.

April 21st.—Cloudy and cool wind from the east. Artillery firing towards Chattanooga again to-day. We have been living better of late, as rations of hams are issued instead of blue beef. Had a shower of rain at 4 P.M. Clear to-night, the Moon shining brightly. I hear a whip-poor-will back of our cabin to-night, the first one I have heard this spring.

April 22d.—A nice breeze from the south to-day. Heard Chap. Miller[40] of the 5th Ky. at the Methodist church to-night.

April 23d.—Received a letter from J.W.L.—Clear in the morning. A strong breeze from the south set in at noon, and now, a few fleecy clouds are floating about. I have been watching their shadows fleeting over the plains, and clambering the sides of the distant mountains.—To-night parson Cavanaugh[41] of the 6th Ky. spoke at the Methodist church. He is a nephew of the Bishop. I don't think he has inherited much of the Bishop's talent.

Sunday, April 24th.—Raining this morning—cleared up about 10 a.m. and I went to church—heard Chap Miller. In the afternoon Prof. Pickett immersed seven soldiers near camp. At night went to Methodist church and heard Dr. Hamilton. He is an intelligent speaker—has a very peculiar delivery.

April 25th.—Wrote to J.W.L. Dull in camp. A nice spring day.

---

40. Chaplain Miller is not identified in Thompson, who says only of the 5th Kentucky that "various chaplains served with the regiment during the war, but no regular appointment was ever made" (p. 693).

41. H. H. Kavanaugh, Jr. Thompson, p. 537.

April 26th.—At night went to the Pres. church and heard a very intelligent man.

April 27th.—A lovely day. Some cannonading in front about noon. Flag-of-truce letters have been coming several days, but I do not receive any. G.P. received one from home, and I answered it for him hastily. He is not able to write well with his left hand yet. To-night at the Pres. church and had a sermon by Rev. Harris, or Harrison, a refugee from Knoxville, Tenn., formerly from Harrodsburg, Ky.

April 28th.—Received a letter from home this morning, by flag of truce. Answered it hurriedly to-night. Did not send the letter written for J.W.L. to-day. A beautiful day.

April 29th.—Cloudy this morning. Cannonade in front. Sent letter to J.W.L., and one home. Received orders to be ready for action. About 10 a.m. the enemy made a dash on our front and captured some of our cavalry. Reported this evening, they have gone back. Went to Baptist church and heard old man Roberts. Rained very hard late at night.

April 30th.—Bright and clear this morning. The shower last night has freshened things up. Showering during the day. At night, went to Baptist church, and as I was coming back heard such a shooting and yelling over at Tyler's (Bates' old) brigade. I thought our "blue friends" were paying us a night visit, but before retiring, I learn the soldiers were tearing down some pillories, which had ben erected in the brigade. The boys call this kind of punishment, "trying to pass the board." Such things would not be permitted in our brigade, as the erection of such "contraptions."

Sunday: *May 1st.*—A beautiful day. Went to Baptist church 10 a.m. and old man Roberts preached a very good sermon. Then Jno. G. and I took a stroll around the lines, which, to right of town, are strongly fortified. In the evening went to Baptizing near Tyler's brigade. Chap. Tomkins of Finleys brigade immersed 25 soldiers. Went to Bap. ch. at night.

May 2d. Cool, though pretty morning. About 10 a.m. received orders to be ready for action at a moment's notice—just before the order came, we heard guns at the front. A few minutes after, we fell in, and marched out through Mill Creek Gap, or nearly through the Gap, and halted in the road. While standing in the road, a cold shower of rain fell, which drenched us to the skin. Soon after, we about faced, and returned to camp. Seeing "Joseph E." on the train, going towards Tunnel Hill, the boys gave him a cheer, which he acknowledged by taking off his hat. Clear and cool this evening. The cause of our move this morning was our cavalry being driven through Tunnel Hill. The Federals immediately went back.

May 3d.—Clear and cool this morning—frost last night. To-night went to the Methodist church and heard a sermon by a stranger. All has been guiet in front.

May 4th.—Warm lazy day. Regiment went out this morning at 8 o'clock, to work on fortifications—to be back this evening. Such a lazy day, I thought nothing would move; but orders have just come in, to be ready in a moment's notice to "go in." Our pickets reported driven in, on the Cleveland road. Reg't came in at 4 P.M.

May 5th.—All quiet to-day. Went to Bap. church to-night and heard Rev. Roberts. Pretty day.

May 6th.—Beautiful day. All are expecting the "ball to open" soon. There is no telling these times, what is going to take place. I don't think there will be much fighting for several days; and I doubt that we fight at all, about Dalton. We may go out to "see" our neighbors.

•7•

We Are Again on the "War-Path": Resaca and the Bloody Road to Atlanta

When the inevitable storm came in May 1864, it swept across Georgia, and swept the Orphan Brigade before it as well. The Army of Tennessee, now led by General Joseph E. Johnston, could do little but resist manfully, stand its ground until outflanked, then pull back to the next good line and try to stand once again. The Orphans faced Sherman first at Resaca, then along the slow road to Atlanta at Cassville and Dallas. At Dallas alone, in a mistakenly ordered assault on a position believed to be thinly defended, the brigade lost almost twenty percent of its men. Those who remained served valiantly, as line gave way to new line, and the place-names of Georgia became engraved in their minds.

May 7th.—Saturday. We are again on the "war-path." I think I shall now have something more stirring to put in my Journal than church goings, and keeping a meteorological table.

Between 9 & 10 a.m. our cavalry was driven from Tunnel Hill, and soon after, we received our orders to hold ourselves in readiness for action—

At 1 P.M. we moved out and took position on a little ridge just beyond Mill Creek Gap, towards Tunnel Hill. Our brigade rested on the rail road on the right (see A) [Map 2] and there connected with Stewart's division, our division extending around to the left to the

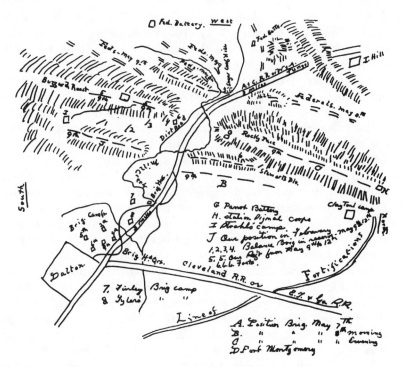

Map 2

base of Buzzard Roost. Lying around all evening, only witnessing a little skirmish among the cavalry in front. Could see blue lines up towards the tunnel, 3 miles off. Has been a pleasant spring day. Twelve at night moved back through the Gap, and formed as a reserve to Stewart, our left resting on the rail road (see B) [Map 2].

May 8th.—Sunday. At 11 a.m. our brigade moved to the right, and took position on top of Rocky Face, as indicated by C on the map. The day was hot and the hill, or rather mountain, being long and steep, we had quite a hard time getting to our position. Sometimes we would have to clamber up places almost perpendicular. The brigade, in single rank, was deployed almost as far apart as skirmishers. The position is a strong one. The hill towards the enemy is long and steep, and is covered with trees. At the top, however, a wall of solid rock rises, someplaces as high as 40 or 50 feet—and in places even projects over. These rocks also rise above the top of the hill, in such a manner as to form a natural breastwork, and thus protects us from shells. The valley, or plain, towards Tunnel Hill is "blue" with Federals. Sherman has a large army. The enemy drove back our skirmishers this evening, all along the line—this little battle, we could plainly see. In the evening, their sharpshooters got close enough to annoy us some. I was sent with an order down the hill to our skirmish line and having accidentally passed through an interval, came near being "gobbled." To-night thousands of camp fires are gleaming in the valley, and the Federal bands are giving us a serenade—when our soldiers request them to play "Dixie," they readily comply, but always taper off with "Yankee Doodle."

May 9th.—Before daylight our drums rattled reveille, and about the same time, our "neighbors" out in front commenced drumming and bugling—making a tremendous noise. Soon the gray light of morning came, and presently the sun rose clear and bright. A mist was settled in the valley beneath and out over the plain and it was sometime before we could see what was going on. At last the fog broke away, and we could see the blue columns marching and taking new positions. We could see for miles up and down the valley, and to the west could see even as far as Lookout Mountain, nearly 40 miles off. Over this wide expanse of country, the fog had settled down in spots, and in the light of the morning sun, had much the appearance of lakes of water, clear and sparkling. At 8 a.m. Maney's[1] brigade, of Cheatham's division, came and relieved us, and we marched down the hill which we found almost as tiresom as coming up. The morning was very hot. We halted to rest at the camp marked I on the map. Our regiment than clambered up Buzzard Roost, and took position as marked 5,5, on the map [Map 2], a wing resting on either side of the battery, or "Fort Montgomery," as we called it. We found this position naturally fortified as was the case on Rocky Face. We could see the fields out in front blue with Federals. They now occupied the little ridge we were on the first evening. Sharpshooting commenced on both sides, and the pop, pop, popping, was kept up all day. The minies whistled freely over the rocks which protected us. Batteries occasionally opened on the Fort, which was shelling the woods below, and often, the shells would strike against the massive rocks, never jaring them. Received a letter from home by flag of

---

1. Brigadier General George E. Maney.

truce, but could hardly get to read it, an assault being threatened. Seventeen Federal regiments were massed at the base of the hill. As they came marching by the flank, across the fields, the sun shining upon their bright guns, the column seemed a stream of molten silver. We had one man mortally wounded to-day, and one had his arm shot off. The night being pleasant, I spread my blanket down on a huge rock, and slept soundly till morning.

May 10th.—Beautiful morning. With the light of day, came the sounds of the sharpshooters' rifles, which have been continualy popping all day. Rained between 10 and 12 o'clock. Cloudy disagreeable evening. Nothing of any interest occured. At dark a rain set in, and continued until midnight. The "Judge" and I got under a projecting rock and with a blanket over our heads kept dry, but could not lie down to sleep. The boys kept up such a yelling, one could not have slept in a good bed. Passed a most disagreeable night. Too wet to sleep.

May 11th.—Dense fog this morning, but soon lifted, and the sharpshooters commenced. In the evening, brisk shelling through the Gap from both sides. We have been expecting an assault all day. About 8 miles off, to the left could see Sherman's supply train moving towards Resaca. The train seemed miles in length. As dark was setting in, the Federals tried to force back our skirmishers in front of Stewart, but failed. Had quite a fight—all of which we could plainly see. The evening cold & damp.

May 12th.—Cold wind from the east, which, being elevated as we are, has a full sweep at us. The enemy commenced moving from our front this morning, to our left, and have kept it up all day. Though thousands have gone, they can hardly be missed from our front. The supply train noticed yesterday still moving & no end to it yet. Sharpshooting and shelling kept up all day, by both sides. Late this evening, they commenced putting batteries in front of us as though they intend to shell us out.—Half past 9 P.M. we fell in, and marched 5 miles to Dug Gap, to our left, where we halted about midnight, and lay down to sleep. May 13th. We were allowed to rest about an hour and a half, or two hours, then we marched towards Resaca, distance, 10 miles. At day light we came up with Cleburne, who was fortified on the side of the road. We passed him, and halted in line of battle, until he passed us, then we moved forward. About noon, we halted, when in 3 or 4 miles of Resaca, and I had a good nap. Late in the evening we moved to the left of the road and a

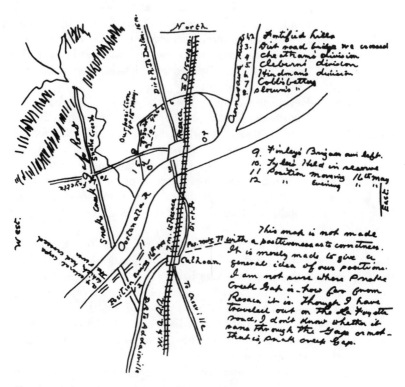

Map 3

detail worked on fortifications all night. We were held in reserve to the balance of the division. Had a good night's sleep.

May 14th.—Early, ordered further to the left. Just before we fell in, rations of whiskey were issued, and some of the boys got so topheavy they could hardly march—in fact, some got so bad off, they had to be helped along. When we got to the position as indicated on map [See Map 3; Map 4], our regiment first commenced fortifying where 2d Ky. afterwards took position; but afterwards we moved to the point, also indicated on the map, and commenced finishing the works partly constructed by Tyler's brigade, which was to lie in reserve. The works commenced were only piles of rail and logs not capable of resisting shells, so we got tools and commenced ditching. By 10 a.m. we had pretty good works; and just in time for about that

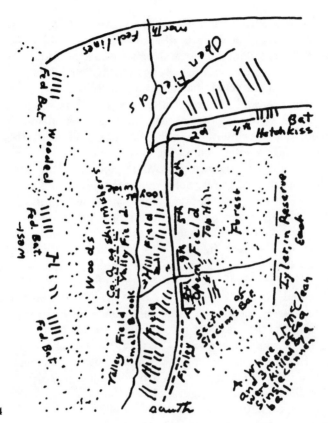

Map 4

hour our skirmishers (co. a) were driven in, the men skirmishing
beautifully. Soon after two lines of battle burst out of the woods in
front of us, and started up, on the charge. We soon commenced "saluting" them, so did Slocums battery on our left, and they retired. A
more vigorous charge was made at the same time on the right of the
brigade, there being several lines, and they came up within 50 paces
of the works, before being repulsed. The day has passed without our
regiment being charged again. Several charges have been made on
the right of our brigade, and in front of Hindman,[2] during the day.
In the evening, the roar of musketry to our right, was quite loud. We
have been kept close by the sharpshooters to-day, having nothing to
protect us but our works. The enemy is on the edge of the woods,

2. Major General Thomas C. Hindman.

three of four hundred yards off while we are in an open field. We could not get out after water until after dark. The artillery has been playing the wilds with us. Several batteries are in our front, on a favorable hill for them, and have kept up a shelling all day. Slocum's pieces being unprotected, he has been unable to fire much—the sharpshooters as well as three batteries against him. Capt. Slocum and a gunner would occasionally slip up from behind the hill, the capt. loading a piece himself and the gunner would fire it, then they would both take shelter behind the ridge. Immediately a shower of shells would come flying over, and would mow down the trees about his guns, but strange to say, not a gun was injured: the sharpshooters, too, would turn loose at him at the same time. In the evening, a battery to our right opened an enfilading fire on the left of our regiment. Company "a" suffered most, as they had to be out on the skirmish line in the morning, and did not have an opportunity to strengthen their works. Lieut. McClean[3] of that company was badly wounded the first shot, and called for the infirmary corps, but had hardly ceased, when the second shot came, killing him instantly, and three men—(privates France, King and Edmonson[4]) besides wounding several. The fire was kept up sometime, wounding several others but killing no more. Company "a" was on the left of the regiment, across the ravine from me, and I was looking at the company (which was lying in rank behind the ill constructed works) at the time the second enfilading shot struck, and I saw the men tossed about like chaff—Seg't Wickliffe,[5] Company C, was killed early in the action, by a sharpshooter. The 4th and 2d regiments have been enfiladed all day by the middle battery (see diagram) [Map 4] and have lost many killed and wounded—at night strengthening our works—worked all night.

May 15th.—Sunday. We look more like standing a siege this morning. Our left companies, over the ravine, have thrown up traverses, impregnable to both shell or solid shot, which will protect them from enfilading fires. Slocum has thrown up works for his battery, and the 2d and 4th have made traverses to protect them against the enfilade.—Slocum opened early, but too great odds against him. Two of

---

3. Lieutenant Thomas A. McLean, Company A, 9th Kentucky. Thompson, p. 808.

4. Privates John M. France, William King, and John W. Edmonson, Company A, 9th Kentucky. Thompson, pp. 810, 812.

5. Sergeant John C. Wickliffe, Company C, 9th Kentucky. Thompson, p. 830.

his pieces were cut down by shot passing through the embrasures. Sharpshooting all day. Had several men wounded, by stray minies coming across from the right. The sun has been very hot, and we have had no protection from its rays. As twilight was coming in, I left the works to go after water, thinking it too dark for me to be seen; but I was discovered, and had a shower of minies sent after me. At last darkness came, and a line of skirmishers was sent a short distance over the works, to watch the movements of the enemy. The Federal skirmishers also advanced out into the field and we had a conversation, at long range, with them. We found them to be Kentuckians, Rouseau's[6] old legion. They enquired for several men in our regiment.—We have not been assaulted to-day. All the fighting was to our right. Sometimes the musketry would roar like they were having pretty hot work. Cleburne and Cheatham to our left, have not been engaged yet.—At 9 P.M., the signal gun fired, and we commenced falling back. The moon was shining bright, and while moving back from the works, company at a time, the men were ordered to hold their guns in front of them so the reflection could not be seen by the enemy. The skirmishers were left before the works, & we moved with the utmost silence. Our brigade got separated from the division before we got into town, and we started to move on the railroad, but halted and went back and took the dirt road. Having lost time, we had to doublequick. Before we got to the bridge (marked 3,)[Map 3] the Federals opened artillery all around the lines and the skirmishers on both sides opened a brisk fire. Times looked a little squally there; but the firing soon ceased, and we continued our march. The road being crowded with troops, we did not get to Calhoun, 7 miles distant, until about daylight.

May 16th.—Rested, in line of battle (see 11) [Map 3] until noon, when we fell in and moved out on the Addairsville road. Soon we were turned back and had to double quick through town, out on the road from Snake Creek Gap to Addairsville, and formed line of battle (see 12) [Map 3]. The skirmishers of the Federal corps which had crossed the river, were driven in, and our lines were being formed to advance and "take that corps in out of the wet," when an order came to Gen'l Hardee, stopping the movement. Sherman with his main

---

6. Jackman is probably referring to the 3d Kentucky Infantry, U.S.A., raised and formerly commanded by Brigadier General Lovell H. Rousseau.

army was pressing too close down the Calhoun road.* Night came on
without our moving, or further fighting, save light skirmishing. To-
night we have large fires kindled, and I anticipate a good night's rest.
We may move, though, before morning. The enemy came into Calhoun about sun-down.

May 17th.—At 2 o'clock a.m., fell in and marched for Addairsville,
12 or 15 miles. The sun rose clear, and we had nice marching before
it got too hot. The country between Addairsville and Calhoun is
beautiful. The forest trees look like Kentucky, and large fields of corn
are on either side of the road. About noon we stacked arms near
town, for a rest. At 1 P.M., the rain poured down in torrents for
nearly an hour. The enemy was pressing Cheatham about two miles
back on the road, and at 2 o'clock P.M. we fell in and marched back
to his support. We formed line-of-battle to the left of the railroad,
and in rear of Cheatham. There were four or five lines of battle, and
we being in the rear line had nothing to do but shift from right to left
or vice versa as occasion required, while the front lines were fortifying "like smoke." "Old Pat's"[7] division was there also—in fact all of
Hardee's corps, Hood's and part of Polk's corps having kept the Cassville road, 2 divisions of Polk's corps had joined us at Resaca. Batteries shelled at long range, but none of the shells reached us. Maney's
brigade of Cheatham's division, had quite a fight, at the "Octagon
house," on the road, late in the afternoon. Night has now come on
and we have fires kindled; and—(as Dr. B.[9] says) have had "spiroots"
issued, which the boys appreciate, after being exposed to inclement

*I see from Genl Johnston's narative that we were simply to hold
the Federals in check.[8]

---

7. Patrick R. Cleburne.
8. In Johnston's official report of this part of the campaign, dated October 20, 1864,
he confirms that it was his intent on May 16 to "fall back slowly," as Jackman intimates
(*O.R.*, series I, volume 38, part 3, p. 615). Ten years later, in his war memoir published in 1874, Johnston says essentially the same thing. Jackman's marginal notation
was obviously not written on May 16, 1864, but was added either in 1865 when he
transcribed his journal or else at some time postwar. His reference to "Genl Johnston's
narrative" is not very specific. It could refer to Johnston's October 1864 report, which
was published in the Confederate press and which Jackman might have been able to
examine first-hand when he was guarding Confederate War Department archives in
April–May 1865. Or it could refer to Johnston's book *Narrative of Military Operations*
(New York: D. Appleton, 1874), pp. 318–19. It is the editor's opinion that Jackman is
referring to the report and that the marginal notation dates from spring 1865.
9. Dr. Walter J. Byrne.

weather.—At 10 P.M., fell in and marched through Addairsville, towards Kingston. The night was dark, the road muddy, and crow[d]ed with troops. We would march probably a few steps, then halt a moment—not long enough to sit down to rest. We were until after daylight marching 10 or 12 miles. Once while standing in the road, one of the men, who had his gun swung across his back, went to sleep and fell back against me, his gun sadly bruising my nose.

May 18th.—Rested at Kingston awhile in the morning, then fell in, and marched 3 miles towards Cass station. The day very hot. We stacked arms and I went to a creek to take a bath. All quiet the balance of the day. I slept well at night.

May 19th.—At noon, a battle order was read to the troops from Gen'l Johnston, commander in chief, stating the time had come to decide matters by a general battle. The order was "Napoleonic" and elicited loud cheers from the troops. They seem anxious to fight. Soon after the order was read we fell in (see 1) [Map 5] and marched

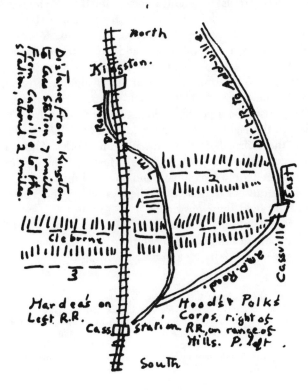

Map 5

out to form line. Our first position (see 2 diagram) [Map 5] was in advance of the main line as afterward formed to give battle. We had only a few shells thrown at us. Cleburne at the same time, was over on the left of the R.R., and his men marched right up to a Federal battery before they knew it, thinking it one of our own. Granbury[10] had to get back in a hurry.—After we had worked awhile at 2 (see diagram) [Map 5] our division marched off by the flank towards Cassville. We marched about the town first, in line of battle, tearing down fences etc., then moved around to the left to support Cleburne (see 3 dia.) [Map 5]. The evening was very hot, and we suffered much from heat.—Gen'l Johnston passed us late in the afternoon, soon after arriving in rear of Cleburne, and the boys cheered him loudly, which seemed to please the general very much. Soon after, "Old Pat" came along, and the boys commenced cheering him. He told them he liked to see them in good spirits, but that they ought not yell so loud—that it would cause our lines to be shelled. About sundown, drew rations. To-night, a heavy detail from the regiment to construct works to our left. I shall now try for some sleep, as there will be no rest for the weary, to-morrow. all looking for a big fight.

May 20th.—At 2 a.m., waked up, and we marched down the railroad 7 miles, to Cartersville, on the Etowah, where we arrived at daylight. We were in an old field near the bridge until noon, before we crossed. The sun was very hot, and the time was not pleasantly spent. We crossed on a ponton bridge. About 2 miles from the river, we turned to the right, and bivouacked on a high hill, at the base of which, on the railroad, is the Etowah Iron Works. These hills are composed almost entirely of iron-ore. Here we found our wagon train, & I immediately took a bath and changed my clothes. "Tis said the reason we did not fight at Cassville was, Hood and Polk declared they could not hold their position."[11]

May 21st.—Slept magnificently last night. All quiet until late in the evening, some cannonading down the river. Sherman, I presume, is flanking us on the left. Pleasant day. Resting up.

---

10. Brigadier General Hiram B. Granbury.

11. Is Jackman's comment about Hood and Polk written later from hindsight? Again, in his October 1864 report, Johnston says the same thing, as also in his book ten years later (*O.R.*, *series I*, *volume 38*, *part 3*, *p. 616*; *Johnston, Narrative*, pp. 323–24). It seems unlikely that he would have known at the time the result of private discussions among the highest ranking officers, and consequently, this, too, is probably a spring 1865 addition.

May 22d.—Sunday. Warm—yes very hot day! and the water being so far off, we suffered from thirst. Church at 10 a.m. In the evening the "association" met near 6th Ky and found several of the members had been killed. I went over to hear the proceedings, and listened to several eulogies on dead comrades, pronounced by different members.[12]

May 23d.—At 11 a.m. moved out on the road towards Dallas. The road was so blocked up by troops, we were until sundown marching 8 miles. Having to stand up in the road seems more tiresome than rapid marching. Had a shower of rain in the evening. Before that, very hot.

May 24th.—At 2 a.m. on the road. After marching 5 miles towards Dallas, our brigade was formed in line of battle across a road coming in from towards the river. Went with company on the skirmish line. We had a most lazy time all day. After taking a good nap, I finished the day reading Miss Evans' new novel, "Micaria." Showery during the day. Continuous cannonading in front. Late, the enemy came out on the main Dallas road, and Tyler had quite a skirmish. About sundown we were taken off skirmish, and joined the regiment, which had moved back to New Hope Church. Marched 5 miles after dark, and stopped in 2 miles of Dallas. Rained nearly all night, and I slept on three fence-rails placed side-by-side, one end of the rails resting up against the fence, to give inclination, so the water would run off. Did not sleep very well.

May 25th.—All serene this morning, both in point of weather and warfare.—At noon moved half mile nearer town and bivouacked near a good spring. About sun-down the musketry roared terribly towards our right (afterwards learned that the enemy charged Stuart,[13] near New Hope Church, and was repulsed with heavy loss). Set in raining about dark. Adjt C.,[14] Johnnie G. and myself made a "fly" out of blankets, which kept off the rain. Slept very well.

On the morning of the 25th, after we had stacked arms, K. and W. of company "B", went out "bear" hunting; but having failed in finding a "bear," brought in a sheep. I don't know how they manage to find such animals—death being the penalty for firing a gun in the rear of

---

12. The Christian and Fraternal Association of the Kentucky Brigade was formed February 7, 1864, as a part of the general revival movement sweeping the Army of Tennessee. Davis, p. 206.

13. Alexander P. Stewart.

14. First Lieutenant W. D. Chipley, 9th Kentucky Infantry. Thompson, p. 807.

the tents, they caught the sheep with salt. W., though a jew, is death on swine. He kills more hogs than any man in the regiment.

Finley's brigade fortifying in front of us during the evening. Brig. Gen'l Finley is away, having been wounded at Resaca. Brigade is commanded by Col. Bullock.[15]

Brig. Gen'l Tyler is also away having been wounded at Missionary Ridge. His brigade is now commanded by Col. T. B. Smith[16] of Bate's old regiment.—Gen'l Lewis is "on hand."

May 26th.—At daylight the 9th and 5th Ky. moved to the left of the division and commenced fortifying (see 1 map) [Map 6]. The morning was very hot. At noon, before we got the works done, received orders to quit work. 1 P.M. the two regiments moved to the right of Finley, and we immediately set to work completing the works, which were nothing more than piles of rotten logs (see 2) [Map 6]. We had not quite finished our defenses—just before sundown—when our skirmishers commenced firing. The minies whistled over us until darkness came on. Shells were also thrown pretty freely. When night came, the regiment was deployed in the works, single file, and two or three yards apart. The other regiments (2d & 4th) had been here all day fortifying. At night they were extended around further to the right, and we had to fill up the interval by deploying. Soon after dark, I rolled up in my blanket and lay down to sleep. Once, the skirmishers in front commenced firing, and we were all up in a moment. The firing soon stopped, and we again went to sleep.

May 27th.—A little before day our regiment moved around to the right, and just as daylight came, we advanced up the hill (see 3) [Map 6] expecting to have a hard fight; but Co. H, in front, as skirmishers, found only a skirmish line, which fell back after a little firing. Our regiment immediately commenced fortifying on top the hill. I went with company "B" on skirmish to the right. Not being fairly light yet, and seeing a line of battle advancing across a field, we first thought the soldiers Federals, but the troops proved to be Vaughn's brigade,[17], Cheatham's division.—Cheatham's division advanced, and took possession of a range of hills (see 4) [Map 6] and commenced

---

15. Colonel Robert Bullock, 7th Florida Infantry. *O.R.*, series I, volume 38, part 3, p. 645.

16. Colonel Thomas B. Smith.

17. Brigadier General Alfred J. Vaughan, Jr.

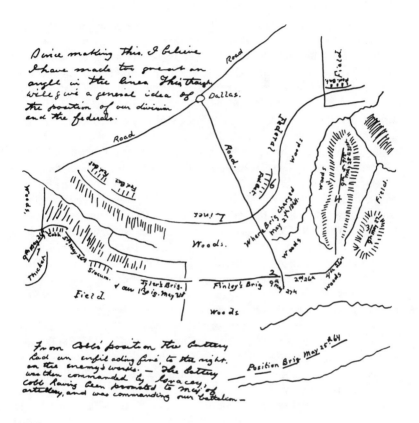

Map 6

fortifying. They only had to drive off a heavy skirmish line, which though, fired briskly as they went back, inflicting considerable loss to the Confederates. About 10 o'clock we marched back to our position on the right of Finley, but had hardly gotten in the trenches when we were ordered back to the hill again to the right. We have been lying here all evening, the minies and shells continually flying over us.—To-night the boys are digging trenches, but I do not see the need, for Vaughn is in front of us, on a fortified line.

May 28th.—Before daylight, clothing was issued to the regiment. At dawn, we move to the position marked 5 on map, and occupied the works which had been constructed by Vaughn or Maney's Brigade, all of Cheatham's division having moved to the right except skirmish line. The hill upon which we are now stationed is very steep and rugged at its terminus on the right, gradually sloping off to the left, the left of the regiment being down nearly in a valley, or a brake, across the hill. We are 300 feet above the level. A. and myself are fortified about the top of the hill. The Federal sharp shooters are very close to us, and keep a stream of bullets coming over the hill all the time. There were some old smooth-bore muskets left lying around by the Tenn. troops, also a box of buck-and-ball cartridges, and our boys have been trying to see who could shoot the largest loads out of them, directing the fire down through the woods, at the Federal Sharpshooters. Some have shot a handful of buckshot, and several balls, at a single load.—Sharpshooting kept up briskly from both sides. We think the Federal Sharpshooters are "terribly" inconvenient, and they have the same opinion of ours. We captured one of them, and he told Gen'l Bate that our sharpshooting is excellent, but that our artillery is "not worth a d——n." Have finished reading Miss Evans' new novel, and think it of not much force.—About 4 P.M. the boys got to their places, and were ordered to hold themselves in readiness to go over the works, and advance on the enemy, at the signal. We took off all extra baggage, so that we would not be encumbered in any way, and waited the word. Soon the musketry and artillery commenced to roar in the valley to our left and front, and the mingling yells of our boys charging was plainly heard. The firing lasted only a few minutes, then became perfectly silent—we knew the division had been driven back, for soon after, our neighbors commenced cheering all around the lines. Satur.—Have just heard the result of the charge. The division was ordered to advance at the firing of signal guns on the left. The guns were not fired but by mistake the troops advanced. An order was given by Gen'l Bate countermanding the move, and aid[e]s were immediately sent to the brigade commanders with the order. Tyler's got the order before that brigade got under fire—Finley's before it got near the enemy's works—but our brigade did not receive the order until it had advanced on the works, under a heavy fire of musketry and artillery. The brigade, alone, was charging the 15 army corps, strongly entrenched. Of course the brigade would have been compelled to fall back, had the order not reached them. The 4th suffered most being on the left flank—(the regiments were reversed)—was subjected to a flank fire, from the troops which would have been employed by Finley's brigade—a battery also enfiladed the regiment. The Brigade is terribly cut up.—Our regiment was not to go forward until the balance of the brigade swung around in line with it, and failing to do so, we did not advance. The boys think Gen'l Bate—"Old Grits" as they call him—went to Gen'l Hardee and got permission to make the charge, reporting that only a Federal skirmish line was in front of his division. The boys generally know what is in front, and could have told Gen Bate better. He "catches it" from all sides and quarters.* While the charge was being made, orderly Seg't Chamberlain[18] of Co. H was killed by a sharpshooter, and several of our boys have been wounded in the same way, to-day. Bright & clear to-night. Has been warm through the day.

May 29th.—Sunday. Have been lying around idle all day. The minies have been singing over our heads as usual from the Federal sharpshooters. The boys have been replying occasionally, with the old muskets before mentioned.—After dark received two letters from home, by flag of truce.—Having rolled myself up in my blanket, I lay down on the side of the trench to sleep. About 10 o'clock at night, I was aroused from my slumbers by heavy volleys of musketry, and the thunder of cannon. The firing broke out so suddenly, that for some time I did not know where I was or what was going on. At last I got my eyes open, and found my way to our "fort," where I found A. already. We looked over and could see a perfect sheet of flame coming over the enemy's works, and the flash of cannon lit up the dark woods so we could see the cannoneers quite plain (see 6, map) [Map 6], and the shell and grape came shrieking over the hill, mingled with the hissing minies. We thought we saw a line advancing up the hill, and opened fire. We soon saw that the lines were not advancing, and commenced firing at the battery, which did not seem to be very

*Genl Bate's official Report afterwards published shows that the order came from army Hd. Qrs & that he was in no way to blame.[19]

18. Sergeant W. W. Chamberlain, Company H, 9th Kentucky. Thompson, p. 849, says that Chamberlain was killed May 14 at Resaca. While it is possible that Jackman, writing from memory in the spring of 1865, might have accidentally transposed an event from May 14 to May 28, more than likely he is correct and Thompson, writing some years later, is in error.

19. Again, this marginal addition is almost certainly a later addition. How much later is uncertain. "Genl Bate's official Report afterward published," to which Jackman refers, did not appear in the *O.R.*, nor are its whereabouts known today. Thompson had the use of it in 1868 when he published his *History of the First Kentucky Brigade* pp. 247–61. Either Bate's report was published in the Southern press late in 1864 or early 1865, and Jackman saw it there, or else he added the marginal notation sometime pre-1868. The former explanation seems the most likely.

far off. We had 60 rounds of extra cartridges to carry, and we thought this a good time to get rid of them. The battery over to our right, threw shells over the hill, which looked very much like rockets flying in the air. Cleburne thought our division attacked, and came to reinforce us—Govan's[20] brigade came up to support our Regt. His men said they were afraid our works would be taken before they got here, and that they "plunged" through creeks and brush, to get here in time.—All soon became quiet, and we again went to sleep. We were waked two or three times during the night, by the same kind of proceedure on the part of our neighbors. Three or four solid shot passed through the works, on the left of the regiment, but fortunately no one was hurt. They could not have fired better in daylight. As to the cause of the firing, we are at a loss. Some say the Federal skirmishers got drunk and turned around so completely that they commenced firing on their own works, and the lines thinking we were charging, open fire. Some of the Federal skirmishers *did* come over to our side, thinking they were going back to their own lines. One of them came upon the works of the 2d Ky., and hallowed out: "Colonel, the Rebs are making it so hot out yonder, I can't hold my 'posish'." He found out too late his mistake, and was captured. After the first firing was over, an officer was heard, riding along the lines, telling that 5000 Rebels had just been captured over on the left, and cheer-upon-cheer was sent up by our neighbors.—As the enemy fired, at intervals, during the night from their works, I believe it was all done to draw our troops from the right. This is only my opinion, however.

May 30th.—Early in the morning we moved to the left, leaving Govan's brigade at our position. The works where we stopped being illy constructed, we commenced strengthening them up. Had not worked long, when we were ordered to our old position, Govan being ordered away. Ferguson's[21] cavalry, dismounted, came in [to] reinforce us. All quiet, save the "popping" of the sharpshooters & the Federals bullets whizzing over our works. There will be a good lead mine down in the valley if we stay here much longer. The bullets are lying around on the ground now, thick as hail stones.

May 31st.—Some shelling over on the left this morning. At noon Stephens'[22] brigade relieved us, and our brigade moved to the left

---

20. Brigadier General Daniel C. Govan.
21. Brigadier General Samuel W. Ferguson.
22. Brigadier General Clement H. Stevens.

and took position in the works first made by Tyler's brigade, to the right of Slocum's battery—Cobb and Slocum have not moved from their first position. We worked in the evening & some at night strengthening the defenses which are not strong enough to resist shells. From experience, the boys don't like for shells to come through the works. Slocum has had two of his pieces disabled since he has been here. The two batteries have been dueling with two Federal batteries "across the way." The Feds have two or more 20-pound Parrotts in position.[23] Cobb's and Slocum's batteries are now composed of six Napoleon guns, each.—Hot!

June 1st.—Every thing very quiet this morning. Don't know what is the cause.—As the morning advanced, we found that the Federals had left our front, during the night. I walked around their works which are very strong. Nothing left but beef bones, and empty ammunition boxes. Some places the bushes in front of their works, are literally mown down by minie balls—done on the night of the 29th May, I presume; and, when our brigade charged on the 28th.—Late in the afternoon the division fell in and marched five miles to the right—bivouacked near New Hope Church for the night. The evening was warm and the march quite tiresome.

June 2d.—Early in the morning we moved a mile further to the right, and formed in rear of Strahl's brigade.[24] Some cannonading along the line, and sharpshooting. At noon the rain poured down, for an hour, in torrents. We could do nothing but take it as it came. At 2 P.M. the division fell in, and we marched 4 miles to the extreme right of the army. The cannon were thundering all along the line of march, and the Federal shells were tearing through the woods about us. Our brigade stacked arms in an old field, and as night came on, I made me a bed out of three fence-rails. Slept well. Clear again.

June 3d.—At daylight we commenced fortifying. After working awhile, Maj. Cobb came and selected our position for Mebane's[25] battery, of our division. We then moved around to the right of the brigade, and commenced a line of works through a peach orchard, near a house—Gen'l Bate's Hd Qrs. At noon ordered to stop work. In the afternoon the rain poured down. At night, slept with G. under a dog-fly. Stopped raining at dark.

---

23. Jackman is referring to Parrott rifles, named for their inventor Robert P. Parrott.
24. Brigadier General Otho F. Strahl.
25. Captain John W. Mebane's battery of Tennessee artillery.

June 4th.—Before daylight, went with the company a mile in front, as skirmishers. Lieut. E.[26] and I took up quarters in a house which had just been vacated by the family in front of the skirmish line, with the intention of setting it on fire in case the enemy advanced, so it would not protect his sharpshooters. As there was a cavalry picket in front, we did not have to be very watchful; so we kindled a fire and "lived at home." K. and W. killed a large pet hog belonging to the premises and while, scalding the animal in the large pot at the spring, the old lady came after her pot and caught them in the act. After giving them a piece of her tongue, she reported them to Capt. S.,[27] in command of the brigade skirmishers. He immediately had them arrested. When the old lady had gone, (being satisfied, as the capt. had promised to report the offenders to the "General,") the culprits were turned loose, and went on with their cooking. Part of the meat, after being cooked, went into Capt. S's haversack, and it is not likely that the "bear hunters" will be reported.—Rained at times during the day. at sundown relieved by company D. When we got to the regiment, the boys were drawing clothing. Set in raining at dark. Am under a barn shed by a fire. We have orders to march at 11 o'clock to-night. This morning after Co. B went on skirmish, the remaining companies were ordered to complete their works, but when nearly done, they had to move, for a Par[r]ott battery to be placed in position. The Colonel would not fortify any more. He said he had given away for batteries long enough, and that if a fight came off his reg't could simply take it "straight." I don't think I can sleep any to-night. I shall "smoke" over the fire until we have to march. Looks "awful" dark—rain dashing down.

June 5th.—Last night we fell in at 11 o'clock, and marched to our present position near Pine Mountain. The distance we marched was only about 4 miles; but the muddiest, and most disagreeable march I have made since the war. The night was dark as pitch, the rain pouring down. I could not see what kind of a country we marched through; but it seemed one continued swamp—the mud and water being from ankle, to knee deep every step. Troops have preceded us, the mud was well worked up. I kept on my feet all the time, but many of the boys fell down and would splash and splatter the mud in

---

26. First Lieutenant Thomas H. Ellis, Company B, 9th Kentucky. Thompson, p. 816.

27. Probably Captain Thomas Steele, Jr., Company E, 4th Kentucky. Thompson, p. 652.

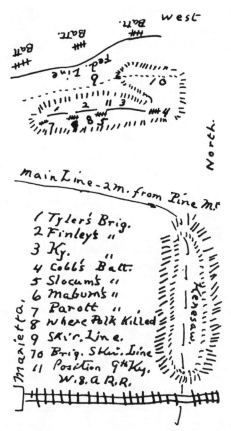

Map 7

every direction. When a fellow would fall, his more lucky comrades would yell out to him to "get up out of that mud—what are you doing down there?" etc. etc. About 2 o'clock we filed off to the left in an old field, and stacked arms. I composed myself to sleep on a log, and never waked until the sun was shining in my face.—About noon moved into the woods, and formed in rear of Cheatham. All quiet in front. Gen'l. Hardee stated the next morning that the march that night was the most disagreeable he had ever made.

June 6th.—Cloudy morning. At noon we moved two miles and formed line on Pine Mountain (see diagram) [Map 7]. Digging all evening in trenches. Rained a heavy shower. Slept well at night.

June 7th.—Finished works. Light rain in the evening. Can hear the drums of the enemy 3 or 4 miles in front—can also see the smoke rising from their camps. The enemy has been comparatively quiet for three or four days.

June 8th.—Cloudy, warm morning. All quiet in front. Wrote a letter home in answer to one just recieved by flag-of-truce.

June 9th.—Some artillery firing to the right and left of us during the day. Light rain in the evening.

June 10th.—Early could see our cavalry falling back, skirmishing. Raining at 8 a.m. Soon after, while standing on the works, I saw the glitter of bayonets in a skirt of woods over the way, and soon after the skirmish line of the enemy came yelling over the field in front. A moment after, the middle battery opened on the hill in front, where our skirmish line is established, and soon after the battery to the right, opened on our hill, being a mile and an eigth off. First the shells fell short; but they soon got the range. The noise of the sharpshooters sounds quite natural. Pine Mountain, and the hill in front, are covered with trees—the line of the Federals, run mostly thro' fields. As yet our battery has kept quiet.—At 6 P., went with the company on skirmish—a wing of the regiment being taken at a time—and our position was in front on the hill (see 10) [Map 7] rather to the right of brigade. Had heavy showers of rain during the day, and when night came on, my clothes wringing wet. Not being allowed any fire, and being cold, I slept none during the night. Our neighbors kept up such a noise, too, bugling, rattling drums, and chopping, etc., no one could have slept in a feather bed, in that neighborhood. A long night—but day at last came.

June 11th.—Rained heavy showers during the day, and it was a weary day. Late in afternon I went out in front as vidette, and two or three from our Regt and myself, with two of the 4th Tenn. Cavalry had some fun getting a party of Federal sharpshooters out of a house in front of us. After the Federals fell back across the field, we had quite a little battle—one of the 4th Tenn. soldiers was wounded in the arm. Late in the afternoon (that is nearly sundown) our Parrott battery opened on a line of the enemy advancing to fortify to our left and the Federal batteries opened on our main line. The firing was pretty regular for awhile, but which passed over our heads. At 6 p.m. relieved by one wing of the 4th. At night slept very well.

June 12th.—Sunday. Am lying around loose. All quiet save sharpshooting. Our division seems to be holding Sherman's troops in check, while our main army is fortifying 2 miles to the rear of us, and Kenesaw Mountain.

June 13th.—Did not sleep any last night, as the rain was pouring down, and I had to sit by a fire all night, with my blanket thrown over my head. Raining all day long—slacked-up at night. Heard locomotives whistling at Big Shanty, which is not very far above Kenesaw. Sherman is bringing the cars with him.

• 8 •

The Hospital Rangers:
After Atlanta with the Remnant
Army of Tennessee

*Pine Mountain is famous in Confederate history for the fall
of Lieutenant General Leonidas Polk. But the Yankee battery
that brought down the general very nearly put an end to
Johnny Jackman's journal at the same time. Shortly after General
Polk was hit, Jackman was struck by a shell and knocked
unconscious.*

*While Jackman went off for months of recuperation, his old
comrades slogged on in the battle lines trying to resist Sherman.
Kennesaw Mountain . . . Intrenchment Creek . . . Atlanta—everywhere
they fought. They almost met annihilation
at Jonesboro on August 31. The brigade was now down to a
mere 833 men, but for two days it fought ferociously before
being almost erased by the enemy. Lewis lost 320 in those two
days. Worse, the campaign for Atlanta had devastated the Orphans.
Numbering 1,512 in May, the Kentuckians were down to
513 when Atlanta was abandoned after the loss at Jonesboro.
Brigade doctors reported 1,860 cases of wounds or deaths during
the campaign, meaning that hundreds had been wounded
more than once. No more than 50 men were believed to have
passed through the entire campaign unscathed.*

*After Atlanta the brigade was less than a regiment in size and
clearly needed reorganization. To make the small number effective,
the army decided to make them into cavalry—actually,
mounted infantry. On September 14, still stinging from the*

fire of Jonesboro, the Orphans were ordered to Barnesville, Georgia, to await their horses. Unfortunately, animals and equipment were in short supply, and the government never succeeded in outfitting the entire brigade. Instead, for months they were split into mounted and unmounted contingents, the latter standing by while the former joined in the harassment of Sherman's flanks as he drove toward Savannah.

When the detachments were reunited, and when Jackman had rejoined the brigade, the war was all but over. Nevertheless, they moved into South Carolina with the tattered remnant of the old Army of Tennessee, still tormenting Sherman. Then in March 1865 they were ordered back to Augusta, Georgia, to meet a threatened Yankee raid that never came. There they were on March 19, when Johnny Jackman made his last daily entry in his journal.

June 14th.—Cloudy early this morning, but cleared up at 7 o'clock. The Adj't and I having made a bed on a brushpile and "spliced blankets," I slept well last night. The sun is shining bright, which is calculated to make us feel lively, after the long rainy spell. Enemy shelling to our right.

* * *

Was wounded a few minutes after making the notes, June 14th, and I did not write any more in my journal for nearly three months. I shall try and give an account of my hospital experience, during the time named, in a brief manner:

About 9 or 10 o'clock a.m. 14th, Capt G.[1] and I were sitting by the col's fire, a little to the rear of the regiment. For two days not a shell had been thrown at our position—and when a shell came shrieking over the mountain to our left, I remarked to the captain, that some General and his staff, no doubt, had ridden up to the crest of the hill, and the Federal batteries were throwing shells at them. "Yes," said the captain, "and I hope some of them will get shot. A general can't ride around the lines without a regiment of staff at his heels." About this time we heard the second shell strike—I thought it struck

---

1. Captain John W. Gillum, Company A, 9th Kentucky. Thompson, p. 808.

into the side of [the] hill; but it had struck Lt. Gen'l Polk.[2] Where he was killed, was not a hundred yards from us, but the trees were so thick, we could not see from where we were, what was going on, and we did not learn what had happened for some minutes. Soon after, an order came for a report to be sent to brigade Hd Qrs and I sat down to write it out. Several of the enemy's batteries had then opened fire, but as we were a little under the hill, I thought we were in no great danger from the shells, which were flying over—in fact we had gotten so used to shells that we scarcely noticed them. I was only a few minutes writing the report, and raised my head to ask the Colonel if I should sign his name to the paper, and had bent over and had about finished signing the paper, when suddenly every thing got dark, and I became unconscious. If I had been sitting erect, when the fragment of shell struck me, I never would have known what hurt me. When I came to my senses, Dr. H.,[3] our ass't surg. and Capt. G. were lifting me up off the ground. I stood on my feet, and not feeling any pain, I could not imagine, at first, what was the matter; the first thought that entered my mind was that my head was gone & I put my hand up to ascertain whether it was still on my shoulders. I did not hear the piece of shell coming, and it was such a quick sharp lick, I did not feel it strike. The fragment probably weighed little more than a pound. It came like a minie ball. After glancing off my head, it struck against a rock, then bounced and struck Col. C.[4] on the leg, but did not hurt him severely. There were several sitting around close together, and they said there was a sudden scattering of the staff.[5]

---

2. General Joseph E. Johnston described Polk's death, being an eyewitness to the event. The generals were standing on the slope of Pine Mountain when a Federal battery started firing at them. "Lieutenant-General Polk, unconsciously exposed by his characteristic insensibility to danger, fell by the third shot, which passed from left to right through the middle of his chest." Johnston, *Narrative*, p. 337.

3. Dr. B. L. Hester. Thompson, p. 807.

4. Colonel John W. Caldwell.

5. Jackman's friend John Green was nearby when he was struck, and later described the scene:

We were sitting around with shells bursting over us when it was evident from the sound that one piece of a shell was coming close to us. Every fellow was holding his breath wondering if that piece would strike him when suddenly it struck John Jackman who was sitting on the ground near me & Col Caldwell & Dr Hester, our assistant Surgeon, & Jim Bemis, our hospital steward. (Jackman was adjutants clerk). He was just making out a report which had been called for by Division Head Quarters. He was sitting on the ground, [and] the fragment of a shell struck him on the head & turned him a complete sommersault. We thought he was killed, but Dr

After Dr. H. had bound up my wound, there was so little pain, I thought it was no use to go to the hospital—my head only felt a little dizzy—but the Dr. said I had better go to the field hospital and stay a day or two, as I was not very well anyway. He wished to send his horse back, and I rode him to the field hospital. Dr. B. again dressed my wound—putting a ligature on a vein that was cut. He would not let me eat anything at dinner but a little boiled rice and in the evening, had me sent to Marietta. He told me that the wound would turn out to be more serious than I thought for. After arriving at the distributing hospital in Marietta, my head got quite sore and painful. At 9 o'clock P.M., took train for Atlanta—Gen'l Polk's remains were taken down on the same train. I slept on a bench at the distributing hospital in Atlanta, the remainder of the night. The breakfast was tough beef, old bakers bread, and coffee that had flies in it, and I longed for the hard tack and corn bread, which I had left at the front. Adjt C. having given me a letter of introduction to his aunt, in Covington, 40 miles towards Augusta, I wished to go there, but my name was put on the Newnan list. At 10 a.m. the train left for Newnan Ga., and arrived there at noon. I was taken to Ward No. 1, Bragg Hospital, Dr. Gore[6] of Bloomfield, Ky., in charge. The room in which I was placed—the Masonic Hall—had about 30 beds, but few of them being occupied, and mostly by men from our brig. The room was clean as could be, and the beds really comfortable. I had been dreading the hospital all the time, (never having been in but one general hospital before, which I did not like much) but I was agreeably disappointed at finding every thing so nice. John J. Woolfolk of Ark., Ward Master; NcNeeley of Tenn., first nurse; Baldridge, of Ark., second; and Smith of Ga., third—all clever gentlemen. "Crawf" McClarty[7] of the 4th, was in the room, wounded, the only one I knew at first.

I immediately went to bed for a sleep, and scarcely waked until the next evening. For several days after being in the hospital, I imagined I could hear the whizzing of minie bullets, and the thunder of

---

Hester, Jim Bemis, & I picked him up & carried him behind a tree; by this time he revived & did not seem very seriously hurt. I poured water on his head from my canteen & Dr Hester washed & dressed the wound & Jack was so bright by this time that we had a hearty laugh at the way he had flopped over, just like a chicken when his head is cut off.
Kirwan, pp. 135–36.
6. Dr. Joshua Gore. Thompson, p. 245.
7. Crawford McClarty, Company K, 4th Kentucky. Thompson, p. 690.

artillery, I had become so accustomed to such sounds. The next day after being in the hospital, had to take medicine for something like intermittent fever—I had been unwell for a week or so. Several days before I got up. My head did not give me a great deal of pain at first, but after being in the hospital perhaps a little more than a week, my wound became inflamed and gangrene ensued, which threw me into a high state of fever. Old Dr. Estell,[8] of Tenn., our ward surgeon, and who was seventy-five years of age, and had been practicing surgery for more than fifty years, soon got the gangrene out, by applying nitric acid, iodine, etc. The fever still kept with me, and the doctor thought I would "go up." Dr. E., about this time took sick, and Dr. Gore prescribed for the ward. He immediately commenced giving me medicine to reduce my system. In about a week, the fever left me, but I was so weak, I could not get up, and had to keep my bed for some time. While in this condition, a force of Federal cavalry came to Moor's bridge, on the Chattahoocha, about 10 miles from town, and threatened a raid of the place. The "evacuation" commenced about dark. All the hospital rangers able to walk, cleared out. There were two left, in my room, beside myself, not able to move. Smith, one of the nurses, and Watson, the ward clerk, were left with us. The citizens all left too. A moving mass of carriages, carts, wagons, "lowing herds," horses, sheep, goats, and people moved through the streets. Soon the town was left, in a manner, desolate. The night wore away, and no raid came.—the day advanced, and though the raiding column was reported in four miles of town at daylight, yet they did not come. Late in the evening, all of the refugees came back, and matters went on as usual.

Nothing took place again, of interest, until McCook's raid[9] came about the last of July. I was then able to walk about in the street a little. That morning I was standing on the corner, and saw the advance of the raid dash down toward the Railroad depot. Gen'l Roddy's[10] Brigade happened to be at the depot, on a train, and saved the town. The raid went around the place, and was surrounded by

8. Dr. Wallace Estill, surgeon of the 1st Tennessee Infantry. Horn, *Tennesseeans*, II, p. 147.

9. Brigadier General Edward M. McCook led a raid on the Atlanta & West Point, and the Macon & Western Railroads, July 27–31, 1864. On July 30 portions of his command were engaged near Newnan.

10. Brigadier General Philip D. Roddey.

Wheeler[11] 4 miles beyond, and the most of the force captured. A good many wounded were brought in town of both sides. We could hear the small arms quite distinctly, which sounded very natural. There was but little artillery firing. There was great confusion in town all day. The streets were blocked up with cavalry for a time. Prisoners were brought in by squads for several days after the fight. The old citizens often brought in prisoners, which they guarded very closely while in their charge.

Aug 10th.—The hospitals being broken up at Newnan, with other sick to be transferred to Macon, Ga., I took train for Atlanta at 10 o'clock a.m. during the afternoon, we got to East Point, 7 miles from Atlanta, where the Macon and Western road branches off, and had to lie over until dark. The brigade hospital being at East Point, I saw Dr. B., and several of the boys from regiment. The sharpshooters were "banging away" not very far off, and the cannon were thundering, and the shells crashing through the woods—all of which reminded me of old times. The train was very much crowded with wounded and sick, and having learned our baggage was stored at Griffin, I got off the train at that place to get mine. I slept until morning on a pile of cross ties. Got my baggage, and took the nine o'clock train—passenger—for Macon, where arrived at 1 P.M.

That evening, J. L.,[12] first sergeant of company "B" and I, went out to the Fair Ground hospital, 2 miles from the depot, in edge of Vineville, which is part of Macon. We were "transported" out in a wagon. The hospital was in tents and being crowded we had to take a tent without any beds in it. Our fare was "awful." A day or two after, Dr. Fox of Ky.,[13] the steward, moved us into another ward. Dr. Jones, a very clever man from Ga., was ward surgeon. We got with several from our Reg't and brigade. I found the attendants very clever.

I could now walk about considerably, and Jimmie L. and I, every evening took a walk through Vineville; and sometimes as far as Macon. Jimmie was a great admirer of the ladies, and would walk two miles any time to see a young lady, even promenading the side-walk. I received attention from several ladies, while at the Fair Ground hospital—one Miss Kate B., a very pretty young lady.

---

11. Major General Joseph Wheeler.
12. James B. L. Lockhert, Company B, 9th Kentucky. Thompson, p. 821.
13. Amos Fox, Company A, 6th Kentucky. Thompson, p. 747.

Sept 4th.—Went before Med. Ex. board, and got a furlough for 60 days. While getting ready to leave on furlough, I took too much exercise, getting my head in such a fix that I had to lie in bed until—

Sept. 12th.—When, though not really able to travel, I went to town in an ambulance, and at 4 P.M. took train for Augusta, via Millen. I got in with some young ladies at the depot, who gave me a nice dinner out of their basket, and when the train was ready, I helped them into a car, thereby getting a seat in the ladies coach. The train, in motion, did not agree well with my head. Thirty miles from the city, my lady friends got off, urging me to come to see them before I went back to the army. I gave a gentleman part of my seat. When nearly to Millin, and late at night, a young lady came in, who could not find a seat, and as I liked her appearance, I woke my friend out of a gentle nap, and the young lady was seated. She was going to Augusta, to see her brother in hospital. We got to Millin at 12 o'clock at night, and had to change cars. By being with a lady, I got into a ladies car again. Seeing a woman in distress, having several little children, and no one to assist her, I was some time in carrying children from one train to the other & received many thanks. I never saw such a jam of women in my life as was in that car. They kept crowding in at every station, and kept up a perfect fighting and scratching. We got to Augusta at day light. I took dinner with Lt. S.

Sept 14th.—Took train for Warrenton Ga., 50 miles toward Atlanta, on State road—5 miles from junction, on Mayfield road. Got to W. at 1 P.M., and took dinner at the Warrenton Hotel. Staid all night at the same place.

Sept 15th.—Not liking the country about W., and thinking it would be necessary to have my head "trepaned," I left on the train for Augusta at 1 P.M. Left A. at 7 o'clock P.M. and all night running to Macon. No Sleep.

Sept 16th.—Took train on the South west road for Americus at 8 a.m., and arrived at A. 12 n. Went to Bragg Hospital.

I again got in Ward no. 1, the same attendants being in charge, save Baldridge and Smith. I also was placed in the Masonic Hall, a large room with nearly fifty beds in it; but there were few patients in the room. All the "rats" were glad to see me back again. My head was hurting me from loss of sleep etc., and I went to bed.

Americus is a town of about 3 or 4000 inhabitants. The business part of the town had lately been destroyed by fire. There are many fine residences in the suburbs. The town, though, while I was there,

looked much dilapidated—the effects of the war. The people generally, were kind to the soldiers—bringing provisions to the sick etc.
The young ladies were "thick as hops," and as a general thing, very
good looking. Being two hospitals in the place, a good many "rats"
were about the streets.

Sept. 22d.—Wrote home. The weather is very hot, and has been
since I have been here. My wound does not seem to be healing any,
and my head is still much affected.

Sept 23d.—Writing up my Journal, which had gotten behind,
since being in hospital. While on the campaign, I kept my notes on
scraps of paper, which I have to-day coppid [copied] into my "mem-
orandum," made of old blanks while at Dalton. Has been a warm
cloudy day—rained in the evening.

Sept. 25th.—Went to church. In the evening attended the funeral
service of Mr. B., a Tenn. soldier, and husband of one of our matrons. I walked from the church to the cemetery, half a mile, which
came near "fixing me"—I had difficulty in getting back to my room.

Sept. 26th.—Being Monday, many ladies at the hospital with delicacies for the sick. From my walk last evening, my head feels crazy
and bad. Wrote to some of the boys. At night an alarm of fire at the
"goober-oil" factory, but the flames were soon put out. I thought the
balance of the town was going to be burned.

Oct. 2d.—Sunday. To-day my term of service expired—three
years. When I joined the army, I little thought the war would last so
long. Went to church. Three churches in town—Baptist, Methodist
and Presbyterian. Episcopal service held at the Pres. church of sabbath evenings. These churches are crowded with women—few men,
save the "rats."

The week past has been very dull. Out of books. Sometimes I would
go to the Court House,—part of the hospital—and read old papers.
The weather has been very hot, which does not agree with me. The
hospital fare is now very coarse. Will be better—so says steward H.

Monday Oct. 3d—Great consternation among the "rats," the "iron-
clad" Med. Ex. Board, from the army, examined the attendants of
the hospital, and the convalescents, sending all who were able to pull
a trigger to the front. The Board made nearly a clean sweep of the
hospital. I witnessed the examination, and it reminded me more of
traders examining stock than any thing else.—In the evening Miss L.
visited our ward. Her sunny smiles, and well loaded waiters, greatly
cheered us.

Oct. 4th—Mrs. R., Mrs. G. and Mrs. D., visited us to-day with well-stored baskets. We had a feast. In the evening Mrs. R. sent me some books.—5th. Mrs. R. sent some books by Mrs. N. and S. In the evening, over in the matrons' room for Mrs. B. to make me a dark bandage for my head, and was introduced to Miss S.—6th.—Unwell. Gloomy, rainy evening. 7th.—A pleasant autumnal day. C. and I went to the river bathing, at dark.—8th.—Being cool, felt better than usual to-day. C. and I walked out to the cemetery in the evening, and I came back with the head ache. There is quite a trade carried on in the streets, selling sugar-cane stalks—5 cts a stalk, being the market price. Quite pleasant and healthful to eat. At sun down Mrs. R's carriage was sent for me and went out to her home 2 miles from town. Had quite a gay time with Mrs. Addie N., a young widow, who came in the carriage for me. Spent a week at Mrs. R's very pleasantly.—15th.—Received several nice presents. Not feeling well.—16th.—pretty day—too unwell to be out.—17th.—Cool—Feel better. Sunday. 23d.—Went to church. Maj. D. and I walked out to the cemetery in the evening.—Monday 24th.—Went out to Mrs. R's, she having sent carriage for me, and passed quite a pleasant week. Miss L., her neice, there part of the time. Also visited Mrs. G. while out. Sunday in town. Monday 31st.—Miss L. visited us, bringing nice provisions. In the evening called on Mrs. E. Later, with Capt. W., called on Miss K.

Nov. 1st.—Mrs. R. and G., visited us to-day, and we had another feast. Capt. McK., Texas Rangers, came in our ward. We "ranged" together at Newnan. Heavy rain last night (1st). 2d.—Gloomy day. Raining. 3d—By invitation took tea with Miss L. Did not come home until 2 o'clock. Had nice time—good music. 6th.—Miss L. sent me nice dinner. 9th.—Beautiful day, which is welcome after the recent rains. The flowers continue to bloom here yet. Have been feeling bad for the last few days. Wrote Capt. W. and Mr. S., rode two miles out in the country after black haws. The ride made me feel better. 10th.—Raining last night. Being clear in the evening rode out to Mrs. R's, and back. Pleasant ride. 16th.—My head being healed, and the patients transferred to other hospitals, I applied to go to the front, tho' not able for duty. I did not care to go to another hospital. Evening rode out to Mrs. R's to tell them good-bye.

Nov 17th.—Mrs. R. came and took me to the depot in her carriage. She also filled my haversack to overflowing with things good to eat. At 10 a.m. took train for Fort Valley. Had to lie over there until

10 at night, then took train for Columbus, Ga. At daylight, 18th, changed cars at Columbus for Opelika, Ala. I staid with Capt. P.,[14] our old quartermaster, (now post Q.M. at the place) until evening, then took train for West Point, Ga. Mr. H. and I slept in a car all night at West Point. 19th.—5 a.m. took train for Newnan, and arrived there at noon. Late in the evening, rode with Dr. B. out to the camp of the dismounted men of the brigade, 4 miles from town. Been a cloudy, rainy day. Slept with Dr. B. in tent. 20th.—Sunday. Cloudy, drizzly day. With Dr. B., took dinner with a gentleman near camp. Felt unwell. The camp is on the battle field, where Wheeler captured the mass of McCook's raid.

Nov. 21st.—Rained all last night. Dr. B. advised me to return to hospital for a time yet. In morning rode the Dr's horse to town, through a pelting rain. Shortly after noon took train for West Point. Got off at La Grange. Slept at the depot all night, and came near freezing, as the weather turned very cold.

Nov. 22d.—Stayed with Mr. K. all day by a good fire in his shop. Saw a few snow-flakes flying in the air. Evening took train for W. Point and staid all night at wayside home, for soldiers. A great home it is!

Nov. 23d.—Morning took train for Opelika. Met J K B.[15] at Capt. P's, also on his road to Montgomery. Owing to an interruption with the trains, had to lie over all day. Evening, saw Gen'l Beauregard passing on train toward Columbus. J K and I slept all night in the capt's office.

Nov. 24th.—We took train at 9 a.m. for Montgomery, Ala. where we arrived at 4 P.M. We reported to the St. Mary's Hospital. Had a good night's sleep.

Nov. 25th.—The hospital being out of wood, we had a freezing time. Evening moved into Lt. O'C's[16] room of our regiment. Nice little room lit with gas. There are 4 beside myself in the room—a Miss. capt, Mo. Lt., and Ga. Lt.; also Lt. O'C. None are very bad off. I don't like the place though, and shall leave as soon as I can get away. This is too much like a penitentiary for me. The patients have passes to go out once a day—those able to walk. If one comes in after being out a few minutes, he cannot get out again during the day.

14. Captain J. Mort Parry, Company A, 9th Kentucky. Thompson, p. 808.
15. J. K. P Burch, Company D, 1st Kentucky Cavalry. Thompson, p. 997.
16. Second Lieutenant Peter H. O'Connor, Company H, 9th Kentucky. Thompson, p. 848.

26th.—Warmer. Reading all day. 27th.—Sunday. Went to Baptist church. Fine church, crowded. 28th.—Getting out of jail in the evening, went to see Maj. D.[17] of our regiment; also visited the State House, and the steam boat landing. Saw several boats start for below loaded with soldiers. Came in at dark, tired enough.

Nov. 30th.—Many patients started for Hood's[18] army to-day. Cool, damp day—disagreeable.

Dec. 1st.—Pleasant day. I feel better than usual to-day.—2d.—Nice day. On levee in the afternoon, and two boats start for Selma loaded with soldiers—convalescents from hospital—for Hood's army.—3d.— Raining forenoon. Evening went to the West Point depot, and saw all the attaches of the Bragg Hosptl in transitu for Hood's rear.—4th.— All day with the boys belonging to the Bragg Hospital, which left for Selma, late in the evening on steamer.

Dec. 5th.—Walked half a mile up the river to the boat yard. Tried how much exercise I could take. I stood the walk pretty well—my head got a little dizzy, but did not pain me. The news of the battle of Franklin, in Tenn.—of Cleburne, Strahl etc.[19] being killed. Fight took place on 30th ult., I believe. 6th.—Visited city cemetery, half a mile from hospital. The grounds are kept in very good order. An acre or two of soldier graves, on a hill-side, seems to be sadly neglected.—7th.—Saw Lt. Wall[20] of our regiment, just from the dismounted men, who, he says, are encampd near Macon, Ga. Also saw Charlie C.,[21] of our company, who is on furlough. Shall start for Macon soon.—8th.—Applied for a discharge from the hospital to go to my command. Disagreeably cold all day. Shall start for Macon to-morrow morning. Am glad to get out of prison.

Dec. 9th.—At 8 a.m., took passenger train for Columbus. Met with B. of the Texas Rangers. We "ranged" together at Newnan. The time passed very pleasantly conversing about old times. After we passed Opelika, the rain came down very hard. Changed cars for Macon at Columbus, a little after dark. Owing to a freight train getting

17. Major Ben Desha, Company D, 9th Kentucky. Thompson, p. 830.

18. Johnston had been relieved of command of the Army of Tennessee on July 17 and replaced by corps commander General John B. Hood.

19. In all, six Confederate generals lost their lives as a result of the battle of Franklin: Patrick R. Cleburne, States Rights Gist, Hiram B. Granbury, John Adams, Otho F. Strahl, and John C. Carter.

20. Second Lieutenant Richard Wall, Company D, 9th Kentucky. Thompson, p. 831.

21. Charles Cecil, Company B, 9th Kentucky. Thompson, p. 817.

off the track, we did not arrive at Macon until after daylight, the next morning, 10th. Finding that all of Wheeler's command had moved towards Waynesboro', Ga., and all the railroad being torn up, and not being able to walk much, we hardly knew what to do. I was, late in the evening, making arrangements to leave the next morning on a train of wagons for Mayfield, 60 miles from Macon, where I could go by rail to Waynesboro', when I met with Dr. Gore, who told me our dismounted men were encamped near Fort Valley. I was greatly relieved.—11th.—Took train at 8 a.m. and soon ran down to Fort Valley. I walked out to camp, about 4 miles, being the longest walk taken for a long time. The boys are quartered in the buildings of a Methodist camping ground. There are about 250 men here, all dismounted, or their horses not able for duty, under command of Col. W.[22] of our regiment. About 30 or 40 of our regiment are here—several from our company. Geo. P. had two truce-letters for me, from home. The detachment from our regiment are quartered in a building—I believe the citizens call them "tents"—made of planks, which is divided off in rooms, each company, or mess, having a room to itself. Though rudely constructed, the "tent" shelters us from the weather, and "ranks" being out-of-doors.—16th.—Wrote to Mrs. R. Have had head-ache several days.—17th.—Over 50 men, being mounted ready for the front, started this morning. Pleasant day for winter. We have nothing to burn but pine wood, and standing around the camp-fires so much—which have to be out in the open air—the smoke is making us as black as coal-heavers. We are living well. Have good fresh beef, fresh pork, flour, sorghum, rice and so on, issued in abundance. We make the molassess into candy—have "candy-pullings" among ourselves.

Dec. 18th.—Sunday. Had preaching in camp—at the "arbor"— many ladies being present. Weather pleasant. My health seems improved, since in camp. 19th.—Very dull. Day clear and pleasant—at 9 p.m., set in raining. After dark, firing of small arms near camp— the boys having some fun, probably.—21st.—Hard wind, with rain last night. To-day disagreeably cold. Lying in bed nearly all day to keep warm—to stand by a fire, was to be smoked to death. Late in the evening, the sun shone out white and cold. Masses of inky clouds about the heavens. Had to show the "Gentleman-of-the-Potomac," the way to the spring, which was done in such a way as to create

---

22. Colonel John C. Wickliffe.

laughter. 22d.—Cold north wind all day. Am smoked as black as a
"nigger." Slept cold at night. J. G. came in. 23d.—Cold. A club from
the "lay-out" gave a concert in Fort Valley last night, and the night
before. Head aching. Gloomy prospect for fun Christmas.—24th.—
Clear and cold. Head aching. Boys commenced shooting, but the
Col. had it stopped. Geo. P. came in at night, off a trading expedition, and played "too much skimmins."

Dec. 25th.—For breakfast had fresh pork, biscuit, baked sweet-
potatoes etc.—Cool disagreeable morning—at noon cold rain commenced falling. Bad prospect for a Christmas dinner—can't cook in
the rain. Slept all evening. Rain pouring down. Has been a most
gloomy day—being the fourth birth day spent in the army. At night,
sat up late chatting around a smoky fire built under the shed out of
the rain. "Dr." Davis, seeing his "christmas."

Dec. 26th.—Cloudy damp morning. Feel unwell did not rest well
last night. Wrote a letter to send home, but concluded not to send it,
until certain the truce-boats are yet running. At night "Dr" Davis
gave us more sport;—"Listening for a voice."

Dec. 27th.—Hazy morning—nearly clear. We cooked breakfast early. Read life of Franklin in "Harper." Pleasant evening. Wrote home.

Dec. 28th.—Last night storm of wind and rain. Capt. G. and Lt.
B.,[23] came in to-day. Cool and disagreeable. Learn the brigade is
down about Savannah, Ga.

Dec. 29th.—Clear and cold at night. Sat up late listening to Lt. B.
"gas." Slept well.

Dec. 30th.—Weather more moderate—cloudy though. 31st.—
Rained last night. Cool all day.

Jany 1st. 1865.—Sunday. Divine service in camp by the Rev. Mr.
Dayley of Marshallville. Very pleasant weather.—2d.—Pleasant again
to-day. Writing, seated on the sunny side of the house. Nearly all
the boys gone to Perry, 8 miles off, to a party given especially for
their benefit. Roll-call ordered. 3d.—Raining—cold.—5th.—Wrote
to Mrs. R. and Mr. McFeeley. Cool—clear.—Late afternoon received orders to rejoin the brigade at Augusta, Ga. 6th.—Set in raining last night. This morning damp, cold. We shall start for Augusta in
the morning.—All the boys out bidding their sweethearts good-bye.

Jany 7th.—A little after day light we took up our line of march.
The dismounted men—over a 100—took the train at Fort Valley for

---

23. Lieutenant Henry Buchanan, Company H, 9th Kentucky. Thompson, p. 848.

Macon. The wagon train, and the men with horses, moved by the direct dirt road—(there are no pikes in the south) for the same place. A great many have to lead their horses, and few have saddles. All the wagons of the brigade are along, being quite a train. We also have a drove of cattle, with us. I am mounted on "Sorghum,"—P's pony,—a little scrub of a thing, my feet nearly dragging the ground, when on his back. When we started this morning was very cold—a cutting wind blowing. The Col. stopped in Fort Valley to draw rations, and a great many of the boys drew too much "skimmins." After the column had moved on, I was back, trying to get some of the boys off. Lt. B. had more than any one else. As we were riding out of town, B. started his horse in a run and collided with "Snodder." Both horses and riders went down in a pile, and I thought Lt. Buch. was killed; but neither horses nor riders, were badly hurt. We marched 20 miles, and camped. Put up fly at night, and made a log-heap in front—slept magnificently.

Jany 8th.—A raw disagreeable day. Twelve miles brought us to Macon. We crossed the Ocmulgee, and found the dismounted men camped on its banks, below the city. Nearly night before the wagons got ferried over.

Jany 9th.—Had to wait until 11 o'clock before we got forage over the river—have 5 days forage on wagons. P. having come up, I turned "Sorghum" over to him, and without much regret, for "Sorghum" trots very hard. Pete[24] and I footed it 6 miles towards Milledgeville, through a cold rain. When we stopped to camp, soon got our fly pitched, and a fire made. Cooked supper. Rain poured down all night. Slept well.

Jany 10th.—At daylight loaded up and moved out. I thought I would walk awhile. Had not been on the road long before it commenced thundering, and soon after the heaviest shower of rain fell I ever saw. Got drenched to the skin. Three miles brought us to Griswoldville, which is nearly all in ashes. The Col. told me to ride in his wagon, which had a cover. Raining until afternoon. In the wagon all day. We passed the battlefield near Griswoldville, which evidences quite a fight. We passed thro' Gordon, (where the Milledgeville road junctions with the Central, which runs from Macon to Savannah), late afternoon, and are camped 6 miles from the place, towards Milledgeville. We have traveled 16 miles to-day. The dismounted

---

24. Peter O'Connor?

men have to march. Our fly is in a pleasant place—we have had a good supper—the night is pleasant, being clear—a fire blazes before us, and we are enjoying ourselves as best we can. The "Judge" is making speeches on the war—so is "Capt." B.,[25] or the "Old Guard," as we sometimes call him—Dr. G. and Booker R. [26]are singing "Kitty Wells," and the "Vacant Chair"—and I have just finished writing my notes of the day.—Expect to sleep well.

Jany 11th.—Up hour and a half before day. Started at 7 o'clock.— cloudy most of the day—a cold wind blowing. "Marched" mostly in the wagon to-day. Fourteen miles brought us to Milledgeville, and we camped ½ mile west of town. The Oconee river is so high, the pontoon bridge is taken up. We may have to stay here several days. We got to camp 2 P.M. and put up fly. As we have been recruited by some boys that we left behind, G. P., the "Judge," Booker R. and myself, all of the same company, have put up a fly to ourselves. Wood scarce.

Jany 12th.—Weather more moderate to-day. Lying about in the sunshine, reading "Love after Marriage." Took a bath this morning and as all the snow was not yet melted off, quite cold operation. Wagons sent back to Gordon for rations. Have a good deal of laugh at the expense of "Trojan," the "Judge's" old horse. He had but one eye, and "Black John" says he saw two buzzards to-day, playing "seven-up" which should have the eye. Poor old "Trojan!"—he seems on the brink of the grave. No doubt his bones will be left to whiten the roadside somewhere between here and Augusta. G. P. and I sleep together. Sleep cold too. A moonlight night.

Jany 13th.—The Judge and I went into Milledgeville this morning. Visited the State House, which we found all topsy-turvy. The desks overturned, the archives scattered over the floor—someplaces the papers being on the floor a foot deep. This was done by Sherman's men. There are some splendid portraits in the Representative Hall and in the Senate Chamber, which are *in statu quo.* The arsenal, standing in the State House yard, was burned. We also visited the Penitentiary which was also burned by Sherman's Army. With the exception of the Arsenal and Penitentiary, and perhaps a little fencing, we could see no further indications of the destruction of property, about the town. The railroad depot is in ashes, and a bridge

25. The "Old Guard" was Sergeant W. W. Badger of Company G, 9th Kentucky. Thompson, p. 840.

26 P. Booker Reed, Company B, 9th Kentucky. Thompson, p. 822.

across a Slough, burned. We passed through the cemetery and saw a fine monument to the memory of a Mr. Jordon.—The country between here and Macon is not as much torn up as I had expected to see. With the exception of one or two houses, only fences were burned. Griswoldville was the worst served—a large factory for making pistols, being destroyed. I saw no dwellings burned in the village—that is no signs of any having been burned, rather.—Our bread gave out this morning, having nothing but rice for breakfast. For dinner we had the addition of baked sweet-potatoes, bought in the country.

Jany 14th.—Clear and cold all day. Had beef and sweet-potatoes for breakfast. Had—as Lt. B. says—"nauthing" for dinner. Reading "Love after Marriage," by Mrs. Lee Heuse. Rations came late at night, and we cooked *dinner.*—The crows were "cawing" about to-day, as though spring were coming soon.—Slept cold at night. The Judge and B. R. kept up a quarreling all night about the blankets.

Jany 15th.—Sunday. Went to Pres. church. Heard good music—a moderate sermon—saw many pretty ladies. The ladies are all that redeems the place. The town is the most ordinary place I ever saw, and in the most sterile country. Has 2 or 3000 inhabitants, from appearance.—Pleasant evening. Helping to get wood.—The boys occasionally go out "deserter" hunting. Lt. B., with a party of 30 men, captured 7 one day. When a party gets after them, Lt. B. says their families have a way of "telegraphing" all over the country, by means of blowing horns. He said he could hear horns "tooting" all over the neighborhood.—Went to town at night—no church. While returning, in company with the Dr., Judge, B. R. etc., saw a sight.—

Jany 16th.—Cool, cloudy morning. G. P., as courier, started for the Brigade this morning at 10 o'clock. The "Old Guard" and I shall sleep together. Shall move tomorrow at 8 a.m.

Jany 17th.—So cold last night, did not sleep much. The Judge and B. R. fussing all night about cover.—Started at 8 a.m., crossed the Oconee on pontoon bridge. By 3 P.M., we had marched 11 miles, when we camped in a pine woods, which soon got on fire, and was some trouble to put-out. I rode in a wagon nearly all day. One of my ankles very much swolen. The boys say I am taking "scratches," being among horses with that disease, so much. The country we passed through to-day not torn up much.—Had good supper of beef-steak, etc. Sun warm in the evening—wind cool. Slept well—put up our fly.

Jany 18th.—Started at daylight. 12 miles brought us to Sparta, a nice little town. The country we have traveled through to-day looks better—more fertile. Besides, there have been no raids thro' it. In town, I got out of the wagon to wait for the "Judge," "Dr." and "Yonteez"[27]—I wished to see them pass through town with their stock. They had straggled far behind. But presently the "Judge" hove in sight. "Trojan" following at his heels with a big roll of blankets around his neck, also the "Judge's" haversack dangling from his mane. "Trojan's" back is too sore for the Judge to ride him. Next came the Doctor with "Edward the Black Prince" following. "Edward the Black Prince" also has a sore back, and is a pretty good match for "Trojan." Immediately after, came "Yonteez," followed by "Wild Bill of the Woods," with a bundle of rags as large as a barrel, tied around his sore foot (scratches). We had a good laugh over the grand "procession."—Camped 3 miles from town. Had sweet-potatoes, etc., for supper. Bishop Pierce called at Hd. Qrs to see Parson Kavanaugh, nephew of Bishop Kavanaugh, and chap. of 6th Ky. There is no danger of the Parson's dying for having too much sense; and Capt. E. says that the Bishop's calling to see the Parson, is something like the sentiment in the song; "Let me kiss him for his mother."

Jany 19th.—Started early and have made it to Warrenton, 18 miles. Camped ½ mile west of town. Just as we got our fly pitched, rain commenced—about 1 P.M. We had turnip soup, etc., for supper. We passed Mayfield, the terminus of the rail road at present, which is intended to run to Milledgeville. Mayfield is nothing more than a station. The country passed through to-day looked very well, yet there were two many pine trees. The frogs in the swamps keep up a "terrible" croaking.—Slept pretty well.

Jany 20th.—Moved out at 8 a.m. Warrenton looked about the same as when I was there last Sept. Has been raining all day. Walked nearly all the time. Have come 15 miles—are now camped 3 miles south of Thompson, at an old school-house. Thompson is a little town on the State Road, or Ga. R. R. about 40 miles from Augusta. Stopped raining and we got supper—had turnips, sweet-potatoes, etc. The Judge, Doctor and "Yonteez," again straggling behind, we ate the supper up from them. They got in just as we were winding up. When the Judge got in sight of us eating, said: "Just in time"—

---

27. James W. Yountz, Company C, 9th Kentucky. Thompson, p. 826.

but he was a little too late.—Raining all night. Our fly leaked, and I did not sleep well.

Jany 21st.—Raining until noon. Lying over for rations to be brought up by rail. Would have been a bad day for marching. Got some straw in the evening to sleep on. Would have had a good dinner but we had no salt to season the victuals.—Did not sleep well, though on a good straw bed. My head hurting me.

Jany 22d.—Started at 8 a.m. The next station below, all the dismounted men took cars for Augusta. I preferred staying with the wagons. Raining all day. Rode in wagon all the time. Came 19 m. At Warrenton, some of the men *mutinied,* declaring they would take the cars, against the orders of the Col. This morning he had the leaders arrested, and is making them walk, under a mounted guard. Slept well. Raining at night.

Jany 23d.—When we started, I got in a wagon and rode awhile; but Pete and I concluded to walk ahead of the train. We got to Augusta some time before the train got in, as the roads were bad. I saw Col. H.[28] and Dr. Gibson. Rec'd. a letter from home, dated Oct. 18th 64. The city has just been flooded from the Savannah river, and is the muddiest place I ever saw. Boats floated on the highest streets.—Camped 2 miles out on the Waynesboro' road. Have come over 17 miles to-day.

Jany 24th.—Have moved 10 miles towards Waynesboro'. Pleasant day. Camp in nice place.

Jany 25th.—Several mounted men started for the brigade, this morning, down of Briar creek. A cold, cloudy day. Have come 20 miles to-day. Camped ¼ of a mile from Waynesboro'. Walked nearly all the way. Am worn out—head aching. Hard looking country, we have come through to-day. Waynesboro' is a most desolate woebegone looking place I have seen for some time. Some of the buildings were burned by the Federals. Wheeler had a fight with Kilpatrick[29] here, not long since.

Jany 26th.—Cold last night. Slept well. This evening, B. R., the Judge and "Yonteez," killed a "bear," and at night, T. and the Doctor,

---

28. Colonel Thomas Hunt had resigned his commission on April 22, 1863, and moved with his family to Augusta, Georgia, where Jackman and other Kentucky soldiers often met him. Thompson, p. 432.

29. Brigadier General Hugh Judson Kilpatrick met with Wheeler at Waynesborough, Georgia, on December 4, 1864, where they fought a day-long cavalry engagement, with Kilpatrick the victor.

went out and "foraged" for a sack of sweet-potatoes. Fresh pork or "bear" and sweet-potatoes will do very well to live on.

Jany 27th.—Evening, the Judge and I went into town. The court house very much torn up. A fine building, and well furnished. Cold at night.

Jany 28th.—Moved back across Briar Creek, which is 4 miles from town, and camped about 2 miles from Green's Cut, on the rail road. Have good wood, but the water is not very handy. Our fly is well pitched, and we have a good bed of broom-sage.

Jany 29th.—Have been sick all day. Have been living too high lately.

Jany 30th.—Pleasant day. Feel better. a part of Hood's army came down on the cars last night, and kept a "powerful" fuss. To-night I hear a violin squeaking over the way. "Music hath charms to soothe the savage breast."

Jany 31st.—Late at night, orders came in for the wagon train to join the brigade at Mill Haven at once. The dismounted men to be left to guard Ray's bridge, 2 miles from here. All the horses are also ordered up—so the Judge and "Trojan" will have to go. I shall go with them, as I wish to see the regiment.

Feby 1st.—Cold in the morning, but as the day advanced, got pretty hot. Started at daylight for Mill Haven, 28 miles distant. As the wagons were heavily loaded, and the roads bad, I rode, bare-backed, on V's[30] old horse. The Judge, Yonteez and myself traveled together. The country passed through, covered with pines—thickly settled. Just as the sun was setting, we got to the brigade. I had not been with the reg't before since last June. Was glad to see the boys. They like the cavalry very much. At night, the brigade had a battle with the "Milish," camped close by, using lighted pine-burs, or cones, for missiles. The boys charged the "Milish" out of their camp and sacked it. They got hats, coats, saddle-blankets etc. The battle lasted for some time, and presented a beautiful sight. At times the air would be full of the blazing missiles, burning like turpentine-balls. Tired and slept well.

Feby 2d.—Pleasant day. Wrote home by flag of truce. The Judge and I messing together. Talking over old times with the boys. Lt. W., a. adj't will get me a horse.

Feby 3d.—The brigade moved for Sylvania, across Brier Creek, this morning. The Judge started with "Trojan," but Col. W. turned

---

30. Probably Captain Phil Vacaro, Company B, 9th Kentucky. Thompson, p. 823.

him back. Col W. came down to stay with the regiment, but Gen'l Lewis has ordered all the dismounted men down here, and Col. W. is to still be in command. The Judge and I took C.[31] of Co. H. into our mess—a disabled man, in the arm. We have for house keeping— one canteen, one little tin bucket, and one round gourd. We have to borrow from the Col. a skillet to cook bread in. Drizzly day.

Feby 4th.—Our camp is on the border of a little lake, out of which we use water, and which abounds with frogs. The frogs keep up such a croaking as to prevent us from sleeping at night, until we got used to them. The pines grow up tall and straight about camp. There is no undergrowth—the ground being covered with wire-grass. A very pleasant place to bivouac. The "Milish" moved away this morning, and C. and I got some of their boards to make us a shelter— the Judge away on detail. We made a very good "chabang"[32]— 5th.—Judge went foraging, and got some sorghum.

Feb. 6th.—"Snodder" and I rode 8 miles into the country foraging, but did not get a thing. Wheeler's cavalry has cleaned the country out. Cloudy, drizzly evening—cold. Dismounted men arrived from Ray's bridge. "Glubber," "Wharf-rat" and "Stevey" of Co. H., and Dick H.,[33] of our company, added to the mess.

Feb 7th.—Raining all day—disagreeable. The new-comers enlarged our "shabang," making the boards. At night it fell down and mashed "Glubber." We were all out by the fire, except "Glubber." He is a Dutchman, and says it came down "mit a bang."

Feby 8th.—Rebuilt the "chabang." Had a good dinner—peas, beef-tongue, etc. Pleasant day. Down at Mill Haven, which is only a plantation, owned by a Mr. Jones. I believe there used to be a P.O. here.

Feb. 9th.—Got orders to move for Green's Cut, and marched 12 miles on the way. Cold, cloudy day. Slept badly at night.

Feby 10th.—Marched 18 miles to the rail road—(Green's Cut), and camped near the Station, which is 26 miles from Augusta. Heaviest march I have made, and if the day had not been cold, could not have made it. Brigade came in, and camped close by. The brig. is now in Iverson's[34] division. Tired, headach—Slept well.

---

31. Probably W. D. Coleman, Company H, 9th Kentucky. Thompson, p. 850.

32. A "shebang" was a soldier slang for shelter usually made of brush or boards placed across horizontal poles supported on an upright frame, with no walls. It was designed primarily for shelter from the sun and not as a dwelling.

33. Richard Hart, Company B, 9th Kentucky. Thompson, p. 820.

34. Brigadier General Alfred Iverson.

Feb. 11th.—One of the company, having to be sent off to the hospital sick, I intend to do duty on his horse, with the company, until he comes back. "Jeff" is a firey little horse.—His wind is not very good though. Received orders to march at moment's notice.

Feby 12th.—Warm, pleasant day. Lying around camp—nothing going on—Sunday.

Feb. 13th.—Late in the evening, our regiment ordered to Stony Bluff, on the Savannah river, 30 miles distant. We moved by the Mill Haven road. Night soon overtook us, and we halted, 10 miles, after starting, to feed. The night was dark, but after dismounting, soon the fires lighted up the pine-woods, far around. As soon as the horses were done eating, again mounted, and rode 10 miles further. Soon after turning off the Mill Haven road to the left, we went into camp, a scout being sent forward to Stony Bluff. Slept well the balance of the night, our captain and I, "splicing" blankets. Cold night. I like the cavalry "bully."

Feb. 14th.—Having still 10 miles to march, we started early. Halted a mile and ½ from the bluff.—Companies B. and H. sent to the Bluff to guard, and the balance of the regiment went into camp. I was left with the regiment to help bring forage to the company. Cold rain set in. Not long after the regiment had stopped, a gentleman came in, and reported the federals crossing 7 miles below, at a distillery. He had hardly gotten through with his tale, when a negro came riding up full speed, his white eyes "bugged" out, (sent by his master) with the positive (?) information, that a corps of Federals were crossing at the distillery. Capt B. mounted the regiment, (Col. C. was left in comd. of the brigade,) and started down to see about the matter. He sent me with orders to the companies at the Bluff, to come out, so that in case the regiment had to fall back, they could rejoin the regiment, and not be cut off. I rode down, and we came back. The rain continued to fall—cold and disagreeable. Sat on my horse as a vidette, out on one of the roads, for some time. At last the regiment came back with the report that no enemy was crossing, and the two companies went back to the Bluff. I soon after followed. The cause of the report getting out about the federals crossing, was, three of our marines came out to get some whiskey, and as they had on blue shirts, the people took them to be Federals—the *three* marines were magnified into a *corps*.

Stony Bluff is a point of solid land running through the swamps, into the river (Savannah). A very good landing for boats. The "Amazon," an old dilapidated boat, is lying at the landing. We are quartered in some negro cabins near the ware-house. To-night have the headache—taking too much exercise. Slept on the floor in a cabin.

Feb. 15th.—Clear and pleasant. Companies H. & B to remain at the Bluff all the time. Head aching. 16th Another boat (the Leesburg) came down this evening. On guard at the landing fore-part of the night. The "Amazon" having wooded—has taken her two days to do it—will start in the morning for Augusta. The old captain is quite a talker. He lives on the boat, having a negro wife; and a niece is on board with him. The hurricane-deck is covered with pet chickens, etc.

Feb. 17th.—Lt. M.,[35] myself, and W., this morning went down in a bateau to the landing on the S.C. side, mile and ½ below, after two prisoners. We came back in the ferry-flat, which has to be pulled up along the banks, by means of hooks. I was amused at old "Ben" the ferryman. He seemed as proud, as commander of the "flat," as if it were a palacious steamer. He gave orders to his colored subordinate in the grandest style. We got a barrel of molasses, which had been abandoned by some commissary at the lower landing—also some peas, wheat etc. Evening, after returning from the regiment, where I went to take the prisoners, Lt. M. and I took a ride in a bateau, on a kind of exploring expedition. Received orders late, to be ready to move tomorrow morning.

Feby 18th.—Joined the regiment early. At 10 a.m. marched toward Augusta. The sun was hot, and I could scarcely sit on my horse all day. At sundown camped, after marching 25 miles. Went to bed immediately.

Feby 19th.—On the road early. March 20 miles—the sun hot again to-day, which hurt my head badly. Passed through Augusta, crossed the river, and camped a mile from Hamburg. Feel better than yesterday.

Feby 20th.—Marched 16 miles to Aiken, where we joined the brigade. Had brig. inspection, evening. Received a letter from home by flag of truce, dated Nov. 13th, '64.—Aiken is in a healthy locality, and before the war, I presume, was a nice place.

Feby 21st.—The brigade marched towards Columbia. Not being able to stand the service, I resigned "Jeff" to another man, and at 4 P.M.

---

35. Second Lieutenant George R. Mattingly, Company B, 9th Kentucky. Thompson, p. 816.

got on the cars, and came back to Graniteville, S.C., (4 miles from Aiken and 12 from Augusta), where I found the dismounted men camped. Got with the Judge, Dick, and C., all in same mess.

Feb. 22d.—Moved camp above the factory. Established ourselves on the margin of the pond, which is very large and clear as crystal. There are two sheets of water connected, of considerable size— nearly two miles in length. The factory is for the manufactory of sheeting etc. Works 350 looms, and 500 operatives—mostly women. The town is regularly built—houses mostly Swiss cottages, or built on that plan, and are occupied by the operatives: it is a "manufac- turing" town. Above, on the same stream, is another manufactory, callled Vancleese—3 miles from here. It is owned by the same com- pany.—The country around here is very poor-nothing but sand- hills.—We made a shelter for ourselves by putting up fence-rails, & spreading blankets over them.

Feb. 23d.—Raining a little.—24th.—Raining all day. Have to keep close to our shelter.—25th.—Cloudy. Took a bath in the pond. Evening, the Judge and I went through the factory. Some very hand- some girls at work here. The factory runs by both water and steam power. They weave 13000 yards of cloth daily. I never heard such a fuss and clatter.

Feb. 26th.—Sunday. Attended the Methodist church, morning and night. The pastor, Mr. Pickett, a great big fat fellow, gave us two very good sermons. I never saw such crowds of women. There are some refugees living here, which seem to be very nice people. The church is built after the Gothic style. The frame work supporting the roof, left purposely exposed—no ceiling. The church looks unfinished—like a barn.—28th.—Raining all day—commenced last night. Went to church at night. The girls are as numerous as blackberries.

March 1st.—Raining—all day. Visited the depot, which is half a mile from camp—(Graniteville is not immediately on the railroad)— in the morning, and in the afternoon visited the factory to see the way "King Cotton" is worked up.—2d.—Cloudy, and drizzling rain.

March 5th.—Raining nearly every day the last week. Prayer meet- ings at the Methodist church of nights, save Friday night, when the Pastor Mr. Pickett, preached a sermon.—To-day went to sunday school to see how the children looked—they were very orderly— and numerous. There is also a Baptist church in town, which I at- tend sometimes.

March 14th.—Our mess moved to the Depot as a permanent guard. We are not to stand guard, but have to look after the commissary and quartermaster stores in the building. The mess now consists of Lt. M. of our company—the Judge and Dick H., also of our company—the "Old Guard" and "Hame-legs" of company "G"—Billie Mc[36] of company H, and myself.—showery to-day. Four or five ladies came out from Augusta this morning, on the train, a kind of excursion party. They soon came back from the village, and took shelter in the depot. They commenced a conversation with me by asking some question. I "rattled away" with them until dinner time came on, and they pressed (?) me to take dinner with them. Their baskets were well stored, and I had a most excellent dinner. On finding out the other boys were my acquaintances, they divided with them, also, the remaining loaves & fishes.—We shall have our cooking done at a private house.—Slept well on the corn-sacks.

March 15th.—Raining until 12 m., when the clouds cleared away.

March 17th.—The Judge and I went to Augusta, on the evening train. We put up [at] the Augusta Hotel. By the Judge's finessing, we only had to pay half fare—$10 each for lodging and breakfast.—18th.—Saw Col. H. and Doctor S.—came out on train at 11 a.m. My lady friends came out on the same train going to Aiken, but I did not know it. In the evening, as the train went back, saw them, and they gave me a large bundle of edibles.

March 19th.—Pretty morning.

---

36. This Billie Mc of Company H is either William McFatridge or William McGreevey. Thompson, p. 854.

•9•

Having Been Absent 3 Years, 8 Months and 4 Days: The Orphans Go Home

While Johnny Jackman went off to Washington, Georgia, to guard the brigade archives, Colonel John W. Caldwell took the rest of the 9th Kentucky to Sumter, South Carolina, to meet a threatened raid, which he could not turn back. The rest of the brigade had been ordered to Camden, and there the regiments were reunited on April 14, 1865. Already the news of the surrender of the Army of Northern Virginia at Appomattox was filtering through to them. Things looked bleak in South Carolina, yet Lewis prepared his men to resist the enemy outside Camden. Driven out by overwhelming numbers, the Orphans destroyed what they could in Camden on April 18 but were still trying to drive the enemy out three days later.

On April 21 they made their last charge. They had hardly begun to move when an order came telling them to halt, then retreat. After retreating they learned that Johnston, their army commander, had formally surrendered in North Carolina three days before. Since they were officially a part of that army, though many miles from it, the Orphan Brigade, too, surrendered. The war was over for them at last, and there was nothing left for them to do but turn in their arms and take their paroles at Washington, Georgia, where the brigade and Jackman were reunited one last time.

This was the last note I made in my Journal.—the old book made of damaged quartermaster-blanks. I shall have to write the balance from memory.

Our dismounted men continued camped at Graniteville until about the middle of April. Our mess continued at the Depot. While at Graniteville the dismounted men were commanded by Lt. Col. Conner of the 5th Ky.[1] Just before ordered away, the camp was moved over on the railroad, half a mile above the Depot, towards Aiken. The number of men in camp averaged about 225. This included all men who had horses not able for service—the camp was a kind of "horse hospital."

We fared well at the Depot. Our rations we had cooked at Mr. Pollaty's, near the Depot—he and lady being very clever. There was a great deal of rain, which we did not mind of course, being under a roof. We fixed a way to burn a torch of light-wood, in the Depot, of nights, and we could read, etc. We became acquainted with three telegraph operators—old soldiers—in the office, and could have the latest news.

Time passed a little monotonously, but we generally had some thing on the "tapis" to amuse ourselves. The Judge was a great source of fun. He was no longer bothered with "Trojan." Old "Trojan" was honorably discharged from service, and retired to the fields of Georgia, to draw the plow—he had helped whirl the cannon along on many a field, and the old veteran bore the marks of hostile missiles. He had served in two arms of the service—artillery and cavalry.

My lady friends from Augusta often came out on the road, and I was always remembered by a bundle of something nice to eat.

Some of the "lay out" gave concerts up in the village, but I never attended. I could see the same fellows "perform" in camp, at anytime.

I attended church occasionally, after coming to the Depot.—About the middle of April the dismounted men were ordered to Columbia, S.C., by Gen'l Young,[2] commanding the Dept.—Not being able to stand a march in warm weather, I made an application for a furlough, which Capt. H.[3] a.a. General of our brigade, took to Augusta himself to have approved, but Gen'l Young had left for Columbia. The "Old Guard," (who was also not able to march), and I were detailed to take the brig. archives—and of the regiment—to Wash-

1. Lieutenant Colonel George W. Connor, 5th Kentucky. Thompson, p. 693.
2. Brigadier General Pierce M. B. Young.
3. Captain Fayette Hewitt. Thompson, pp. 476–77.

ington, Ga. We preferred this to going to a hospital. We were to stay at W. until further orders. We remained at Graniteville two or three days after the comd had marched. The "Old Guard" had fallen in love with a widow, and wished to stay a few days longer.

On the 17th day of April, the "Old Guard" and I took train for Augusta, in the morning, having in charge several boxes of books, papers, etc. Before starting, while on our way to Augusta, one of our "telegraph" friends told me that some very bad news had come over the wires, but would not tell me what it was. At 7 o'clock P.M., we took passenger train for Barnett, 58 miles up toward Atlanta, where the road branches off to Washington, Ga. Met with Col. H. on the train. We got off at Barnett about 2 o'clock at night, and slept in a freight car until morning. Barnett is only a station at the Junction of the Washington road. We had to lie over until 2 P.M., the 18th.— Gen'l Hood came down on the train from Washington, and took the up train for Atlanta at 12 m. He must have known of Lee's surrender, for he looked very "blue."

At 2 P.M. the train left for Washington, and being only 18 miles to run, we soon got there. We immediately went to the building where a detail from our brigade was making saddles. We remained with the detail all the time. I carried water for C. to cook with, and the "Old Guard" cut wood—by this means we had our cooking done; we drew rations with the detail. We stored the boxes in the same building. I amused myself by writing most of the time. Wrote the first 6 months of my Journal from memory and copied from the little memorans book the notes of each day so far as kept after Mch 30th, 1862. We slept on the floor, which suited us very well—what we were used to. There were about 15 or 20 men at work at saddlery. They put up a very nice, and substantial saddle.

Washington is a town of about 2000 inhabitants. It is well built, and in a better country than usual, for Georgia. There are some nice residences in the place—that of "Bob Tooms"[4] is the finest dwelling in town. The inhabitants are very aristocratic.

We had not been at Washington but a few days, when Lee's paroled men commenced coming through. From that time on, the streets were full of soldiers. They were straggling into town all the time, coming across from Abbeville S.C.—By coming this route, they had only about 50 miles to walk.

---

4. Robert Toombs, former U.S. Senator and Confederate Secretary of State.

At last the news came of the surrender of Johnston. We knew then, that we had "gone up."

One evening the 8th Texas Cavalry—"the Rangers"—came through town, making their way west of the Chattahoocha. They "charged" the com depot, at the Court House, for forage. They then got the straggling soldiers into a Q.M.'s department, and they threw out writing paper, thread, buttons, etc., on the streets, by the wagon load. The little negroes and citizens soon had wheel-barrows on the ground to take the plunder home. After the "Rangers" had gone, the Q.M. had a guard to stop the pillagers. The guards were chasing the little negroes about for some time, on the streets, making them "shell out" the stolen goods.

The next day, Ferguson's[5] brigade came through, and they "charged" around considerably, but all the government stores were about gone before they came in.—At the Depot were piles of ammunition, which the little boys and citizens carried away as much as they wished. I expected to see the Depot blown up, by carelessness.

I believe it was in the afternoon of May 3d "Uncle Jeff"[6] rode into town escorted by company B of the 2d Ky. cavalry—Gen'l Duke's[7] old regiment. He had on a broad brimmed, light colored felt hat, which had a wide stripe of black crepe around the crown, & the brim turned down. He wore a gray coat without any gold-lace on it (but I think it was cut in military style), and he had on gray pants, which were stuffed into a pair of cavalry boots. I had never seen him dressed in this style before, but I knew him the moment I saw him. He dismounted at the old bank-building, on the public square, near where we were staying. Nearly all of his cabinet were with him. Dr. ——, the banker, entertained him.[8] Many citizens called on the President.

The next morning, Gen'l Bragg came into town, and about 9 a.m. he and the President rode away alone, going back towards Abbeville—or started out that street at least.[9] The Cabinet, here left the President—or they separated rather—and the Confederate government ceased to exist.

---

5. Brigadier General Samuel W. Ferguson.
6. Jefferson Davis arrived in Washington on the morning of May 3. Burke Davis, *The Long Surrender* (New York, 1985), p. 126.
7. Brigadier General Basil W. Duke.
8. Dr. J. J. Robertson, cashier of the Bank of Georgia, gave Davis lodgings. Davis, *Surrender*, p. 126.
9. Jefferson Davis left Washington at 10 A.M. Davis, *Surrender*, p. 128.

That afternoon, Gen'l Breckinridge, Secretary of War, came into town and staid all night at the same place Pres. Davis had lodged. Before leaving town, he sent an order to Duke's brigade, which had passed through in the morning, to surrender—that the department had been surrendered by Johnston. This was the last order issued by the authority of the Confederate government.

The following morning, Breckinridge left town, and in the evening, a company of Federal cavalry came in, and took charge of affairs.

The next evening, May 6th the brigade came to Washington. As they marched through the streets, coming in from one direction, all armed, and their flags flying, they passed the 13th Tenn Federal Cavalry, coming from the opposite direction. It looked strange not to see them commence shooting at each other. I worked until 10 o'clock at night getting up the proper papers for the regiment to be paroled. At 2 o'clock at night the regiment was paroled.—The Federal Provost Marshal worked nearly all night paroling us. This was the 6th of May. The next day all the brigade was paroled, and we "broke up house-keeping."—each fellow being free to wander off, as his inclinations led him, with his horse, saddle and bridle.

May 8th.—I went to Augusta, and a few days after nearly all the regiment met there. We expected to go around by water *via* Savannah; but we gave out such a trip, and all started up by Atlanta. Not being able to travel much, I got off the train, with a friend, at Union Point, near Greensburg, Ga., and went out near White Plains, to stay until the railroad repairs were completed from Atlanta to Chattanooga. We stopped with Mr. Wright, a clever old planter (and old Mrs. W. was a very kind old lady)—about 2 miles from the Plains. Here we stayed until the latter part of the month, amusing ourselves fishing, and other sports were gotten up for our entertainment. I never visited the Plains—only a post office. There were two others of the brigade in the neighborhood, and we all started for home together, being four in the party.—We were all crippled, and disabled by wounds recd in the service.

At last, about the latter part of May, learning the railroad between Atlanta and Chattanooga was about done, we bade our friends good-bye, and in a carriage, came to Union Point, 12 miles, to take the cars. At 1 P.M. the train for Atlanta came along, and we "bounced" it. Eight miles above, at Greensburg, our two other companions came aboard. We got to the ruins of Atlanta late at night, and slept under a shade tree until morning.

The next day, finding 60 miles, or more, of the road not completed, we bargained with a Federal, who had two wagons under his charge, going through to Resaca, to take us over the road. We left Atlanta at 1 P.M. Atlanta looked desolate, having been burned, since I had last seen it. We camped at Marietta at night. This town, we also found in ruins.

The next day we came as far as Acworth.—

The day after, we passed through Cartersville, on the Etowah, and Cassville, which was in complete ruins. In the evening we got to Addairsville, and took the train for Dalton. The road had just been finished to A-ville., and we came up on the construction train. The employees seemed disposed to show us favors. We bivouacked near the Depot at Dalton for the night—got there about 10 o'clock P.M. Cold night. Last time I slept on the ground.

The next morning the train, which was flat cars, left for Chattanooga. Got into Chattanooga at noon. Being quite a number of Confeds along, we could not get transportation that day. At night we put up at the Soldiers' Home, "Yank" and "Confed" eating out of the same platter, and cracking jokes at each other, as though they had never met in many a mortal combat.

The next evening we took train for Nashville, and by day light, or a little after, the next morning, we were in that city.

This was May 29th. We were all marched—not under guard—to the Provost Marshal's office, and then informed that the Kentuckians could not go home unless first taking the amnesty oath, and we were "galvanized."[10] I did not care to wait for Government transportation by water, so that evening, at 3 o'clock, I took the train for Louisville having to pay my passage, and at 7 o'clock at night, got off at Bardstown Junction. Rather than wait until the following evening for the train, I immediately started on foot up the rail road, and got home about 10 a.m. the 30th of May, having been absent, 3 years, 8 months and 4 days.—

---

10. On May 29, 1865, Jackman appeared before First Lieutenant William H. Bracken, Assistant Provost Marshal General of the Department of the Cumberland, in Nashville, and swore the oath of allegiance. Jackman, Service Record.

Index